NEW TESTAMENT MESSAGE

A Biblical-Theological Commentary

Wilfrid Harrington, O.P. and Donald Senior, C.P.

EDITORS

New Testament Message, Volume 16

1 and 2
THESSALONIANS

James M. Reese, O.S.F.S.

Michael Glazier, Inc.
Wilmington, Delaware

MICHAEL GLAZIER, INC.
1210A King Street
Wilmington, Delaware 19801

Library of Congress Catalog Card Number: 79-53889
International Standard Book Number
New Testament Message series: 0-89453-123-9
1 & 2 THESSALONIANS: 0-89453-139-5

Printed in the United States of America by Abbey Press

CONTENTS

EDITORS' PREFACE

New Testament Message is a commentary series designed
to bring the best of biblical scholarship to a wide audience.
Anyone who is sensitive to the mood of the church today is
aware of a deep craving for the Word of God. This interest
in reading and praying the scriptures is not confined to a
religious elite. The desire to strengthen one's faith and to
mature in prayer has brought Christians of all types and all
ages to discover the beauty of the biblical message. Our age
has also been heir to an avalanche of biblical scholarship.
Recent archaeological finds, new manuscript evidence, and
the increasing volume of specialized studies on the Bible
have made possible a much more profound penetration of
the biblical message. But the flood of information and its
technical nature keeps much of this scholarship out of the
hands of the Christian who is eager to learn but is not a
specialist. *New Testament Message* is a response to this
need.

The subtitle of the series is significant: "A Biblical-
Theological Commentary." Each volume in the series, while
drawing on up-to-date scholarship, concentrates on bringing to the fore in understandable terms the specific message of each biblical author. The essay-format (rather than
a word-by-word commentary) helps the reader savor the
beauty and power of the biblical message and, at the same
time, understand the sensitive task of responsible biblical
interpretation.

A distinctive feature of the series is the amount of space
given to the "neglected" New Testament writings, such as
Colossians, James, Jude, the Pastoral Letters, the Letters

of Peter and John. These briefer biblical books make a significant but often overlooked contribution to the richness of the New Testament. By assigning larger than normal coverage to these books, the series hopes to give these parts of Scripture the attention they deserve.

Because *New Testament Message* is aimed at the entire English speaking world, it is a collaborative effort of international proportions. The twenty-two contributors represent biblical scholarship in North America, Ireland, Britain and Australia. Each of the contributors is a recognized expert in his or her field, has published widely, and has been chosen because of a proven ability to communicate at a popular level. And, while all of the contributors are Roman Catholic, their work is addressed to the Christian community as a whole. The New Testament is the patrimony of all Christians.It is the hope of all concerned with this series that it will bring a fuller appreciation of God's saving Word to his people.

Wilfrid Harrington, O.P.
Donald Senior, C.P.

Introduction

THE SCHEMA of Paul's three missionary journeys in Acts of the Apostles is a literary oversimplification of his complicated missionary career. Yet it provides a helpful framework for dealing with Paul's letters. He came into Europe on the second journey after winning approval from the Jerusalem christian community that converts from paganism should not be treated as second-class christians (cf. Acts 15:22-29).

According to Acts Paul decided to make his preaching headquarters in Asia Minor but was directed in a dream to evangelize Europe. This led to his preaching in Philippi and then in Thessalonica (cf. Acts 16:6-17:9). Acts gives only a sketchy picture of his work there and of the opposition it generated. At Thessalonica he was able to establish a community made up principally of pagan converts (cf. 1 Thess 1:9).

The City and Paul's Visit

Thessalonica was founded by Cassander, a general of Alexander the Great, by bringing together inhabitants of 26 villages in the region into this strategic location on the Thermaic Gulf of the Aegean Sea in 314 B.C. He named it in honor of his wife, Alexander's half-sister. After the Romans definitively annexed it in 146 B.C., they made it capital of their province of Macedonia. At the time of Paul's visit it was the second largest city of Greece and seat of a Roman proconsul.

When Paul arrived there about 50 A.D., Thessalonica had an important Jewish community with its synagogue.

His preaching converted to the christian faith some of the godfearing pagans who frequented this synagogue. Their defection aroused Jewish anger against Paul, and for his safety the christians sent him away secretly (cf. Acts 17:1-10). Acts gives the impression that Paul was in the city only a few weeks, but the contents of 1 Thess points to a longer stay—Rigaux judges a few months (cf. 1 Thess 2:9).

How large the christian community was at the time Paul wrote to them is impossible to determine, but indications from the two letters point to a fairly large church with diverse groups that had their own identity (cf. 1 Thess 4:11-12; 5:12-15; 2 Thess 3:6-11). The situations and problems that elicited these letters are intimately linked to Paul's method of writing to the community and will be treated within this commentary.

Opposition to this new religious group continued after Paul had been sent away. He heard about it and sent Timothy there to report to him. Timothy was a young companion of Paul, son of a pagan father and a Jewish mother. Paul had him circumcised so that he would be able to work with Jews (Acts 16:1-3). Paul's first apostolic letter is a response to the report of Timothy about conditions in this christian community that was still less than a year old. No doubt Timothy took the letter back and elaborated upon it to clarify Paul's teaching and to encourage community members to persevere in their new faith.

Content and Style of First Thessalonians

Paul had been a christian for about 15 years and an itinerant missionary among pagans of Asia Minor and Greece for several years when he made his decision to write this letter. It was an important decision because it is the historical origin of the New Testament as the liturgical library of the apostolic church. Paul wrote at the height of his highly successful mission of establishing the church at Corinth. He could not leave this work to deal with the problems faced by the Thessalonian christians. His letter is both an authoritative apostolic statement and a liturgical document, that is, it was meant to be proclaimed in the prayerful setting of community worship.

In composing this letter Paul developed the shaping principle of the apostolic letter as one of the literary forms of the New Testament community. He begins by gathering the members of the Thessalonian community together with him in an expression of thanksgiving to God for their fruitful faith, for the affectionate concern generated by their new life together and for the hope that continued to nourish perseverance in Christ. Much of the letter is simply a recalling of the joyful experience of faith and hope they had received and shared generously with their fellow Macedonians. Paul writes this way to involve them more deeply in his personal desire to praise God as their savior. He knows that the best way to kindle their intense religious experience is to recall what God did for them.

Next Paul spends a portion of the letter reminding them of his personal affection and concern—even his manual labor—so as not to be a burden to them (2:1-20). He wanted to hear about them so much that he sacrificed even the presence and support of Timothy to find out how they were faring in the faith (3:1-8). Only when he has renewed the deep bonds between them and himself does Paul turn to the necessary task of clarifying their understanding about christian faith and lifestyle (3:9-5:11). Even in this instruction Paul deals with them gently, acting the part of the professional 'nurse' when she nurses her own child (cf. 2:7).

The tone of this first letter of Paul is warm and tender, encouraging them without indulging any of their faults. The Thessalonians had grown close to Paul while he lived with them. At the same time the questions raised show that he did not have time to finish off the basic doctrinal and moral instructions that these former pagans needed to adopt a total christian lifestyle. His instructions fall into three areas: (1) questions of faith in the return of Jesus; (2) the exercise of mutual love within the community; (3) the need for personal moral integrity or holiness as the condition for enjoying a part in the glory of Jesus at his return (cf. 3:9-13).

The mere listing of these topics cannot do justice to the way Paul handles them. The commentary will call attention to Paul's pastoral skill in aspects of the communication process. The imparting of information was only a small part of Paul's message.

Special Problems about Second Thessalonians

Chiefly because of the content of 2 Thess 2:1-10, the authenticity of this letter has been challenged by many critics. That paragraph contains an attack on "overrealized eschatology," that is, the belief that the return of the Lord Jesus is already here. Paul rejects this teaching and recalls how he explained to them that Jesus would not return until the coming of the apostasy and the revelation of the *'man of lawlessness.'* These events cannot occur until *'he who now restrains'* the *'mystery of lawlessness'* is out of the way. The difficulty for modern readers is that this is the only mention of the mysterious apocalyptic drama in the letters of Paul.

Even without understanding these events, Gerhard Krodel argues, the message of this paragraph goes in the opposite direction to 1 Thess 4:13-5:11, namely, the proclamation of the imminent return of Jesus. While it is true that no one can say with certainty what event Paul refers to in this paragraph, it is also true that vagueness of language is a feature of apocalyptic style, which does not spell out its allusions. Krodel and others commit the methodological fallacy of conceptualizing the imagery of this passage. Apocalyptic writing cannot be read like logical narration. In reality, the conflicts between images of the parousia in these two letters is not greater than conflicts within the same apocalyptic discourse in Mk 13:5-37.

Further arguments against the authenticity of 2 Thess are based on the claim that a forger copied phrases from

1 Thess. Yet a careful comparison of the alleged passages shows awareness of the existence of 1 Thess but not a slavish copying of phrases from it. No adequate explanation has been offered why a forger should have produced 2 Thess. Those who argue for its non-Pauline origin have not provided a satisfactory motive for its existence.

Other attempts to explain the relationship between these two letters—such as seeing 2 Thess as the earlier one or as addressed to a different part of the community than 1 Thess—have failed to shed light on this unsolved problem. The solution adopted here implies that 2 Thess reveals Paul as still struggling with his responsibility as an apostle but not yet in complete control of his mode of expression. Many gaps still exist in our knowledge of early Pauline communities. It is imprudent to fill in these gaps by conjecture and then to interpret Paul's letters in terms of such proposals.

Message of the Letters to the Thessalonians

These early letters of Paul paint in broad strokes the eschatological nature of christian faith. The horizons of the new life given by God in Jesus are faith, mutual love and the hope of the return of Jesus as Lord (cf. 1 Thess 1:3; 2 Thess 1:3-4). Christian life is a call by God to prepare for sharing in the victory of Jesus by growing in these gifts and by becoming a witness to the holiness imparted 'in Christ.' The message of these letters is communicated prayerfully as fruit of Paul's own life in Christ and as an expression of his apostolic concern for those he invited to believe. Hence, they can be understood only in the climate of prayer and confidence in God's promise to complete Christ's work. In addition, these are the most apocalyptic of Paul's extant letters both in outlook and in style and so make special demands upon modern readers.

They reveal the heart of Paul—father, nurse, apostle, fellow-believer, one who builds up and encourages those under attack (cf. 1 Thess 2:17; 3:5-10; 4:1). He does not develop at great length any abstract doctrine in these short letters but rather communicates the joy of the new life in the spirit received from the Lord Jesus Christ, who is already the center of community faith.

In keeping with the nature and style of these letters as celebrations of thanksgiving and words of encouragement and instruction, this commentary does not attempt to paraphrase their informational content. Rather it guides readers into a deeper appreciation of the way Paul unfolds his message. Thus it will often indicate the literary techniques Paul employs to communicate his desires for the community. Content will be explained when his terminology is technical or otherwise unclear to modern readers. Often, today's reader will find more encouragement in the spirit with which Paul supports this young community than in lengthy explanations of background details.

A fruitful reading of these letters demands creative activity on the part of modern believers to identify both with the concern of Paul and with the uncertainty manifest in their original readers. Above all, modern men and women must make the additional step of translating the message of these letters into contemporary situations. Technical information available in more elaborate commentaries can assist in this translation but cannot replace reader-involvement in the concerns of Paul. What this commentary will point out at appropriate places is the development of the discourse structure, the unfolding of the message. Paul was faced with a concrete set of needs and dealt with them in an intensely personal way. He seldom theorized. Yet a profound religious experience and vision became incarnate in his response. It remains to be appropriated as each generation reads this great apostle in new historical situations.

1 THESSALONIANS

1 Thessalonians

PAUL GREETS THE COMMUNITY.
1 Thess 1:1.

> **1** Paul, Silvanus, and Timothy,
> To the church of the Thessalonians in God the Father
> and the Lord Jesus Christ:
> Grace to you and peace.

THIS IS the address, the first and necessary element common to all Greek letters at the time Paul writes. But he does not take it over untouched. Paul modified even this stereotyped feature and adapted it to his apostolic purpose. His decision to write to this young christian community that he had founded only a few months before was crucial in church history. It led eventually to the formation of the small library of writings that would later be gathered together as the sacred writings of the new covenant—the New Testament. Paul now makes writing an extension of his authority as an apostle of Jesus Christ.

'Paul' as a personal name appears only in the New Testament and writings dependent upon Paul. It is a nickname, a transliteration of the Latin word meaning "short." Yet this is the name Paul uses to identify himself. He does not add any title to further designate himself. He imagines himself in their midst as a fellow worshiper of God. He does not want to present himself as one apart, commanding them. This simplicity reflects his sense of being a fellow member of the believing group now gathered at Thessalonica. Paul joins them in spirit and for the first time in his missionary career undertakes to create a community by means of an apostolic letter.

3

Paul's use of the plural *'we'* throughout most of this letter expresses his bond of unity with his fellow missionaries *'Silvanus'* and *'Timothy.'* It does not mean that they helped him compose the letter as a common project. His slipping into the singular in 2:18; 3:5, and 5:27 points to Paul as the sole literary author.

'Silvanus' is the Silas chosen by Paul as his companion for the second missionary journey after the split with Barnabas (Acts 15:36-40). Silas played an active part in that journey but is not mentioned again in Acts after his arrival in Corinth (Acts 18:5). He appears as the secretary involved in writing the first letter of Peter (1 Pt 5:12).

Acts describes the arrival of Paul and Silas in Thessalonica, Paul's preaching in the synagogue for three weeks, and the conversion of some Jews and many god-fearing Hellenists. Seeing this success, envious Jews gathered a mob, stirred up the city and tried to seize Paul at the home of his host Jason. When they did not find Paul, they took Jason and some believers to the city authorities and accused them of acting against the Roman government. Frightened by this, the christians immediately sent Paul and Silas away into Beroea, where they again started to preach the good news (Acts 17:1-10).

'Timothy' was a christian from Lystra, son of a Jewish-christian mother and a Greek father. Paul took him along as companion during his second journey through Asia Minor (Acts 16:1-5). Acts does not mention Timothy during Paul's stay at Thessalonica, perhaps because of his subordinate role. Yet Timothy must have been at Thessalonica. Later in this letter Paul recalls that he sent him from Athens to look into conditions in the community and to *'exhort you'* (3:2). No doubt it is Timothy who carries this letter from Corinth and reads it to the assembled group on Paul's behalf. According to the account in Acts, Timothy stayed with Silas at Beroea when Paul was forced to flee that city. Paul gave instructions that they were to join him at Athens as soon as possible (Acts 17:14-15).

Paul addresses this letter to the whole *'church,'* that is, to the entire group of people who had accepted his preaching and put their trust in the salvation promised by God in and through the risen Jesus Christ. The Greek word *ekklesia* translates the Hebrew term for the sacred assembly of the chosen people. The number of members at this time was probably small enough to fit into a single meeting room.

This group was a small part of the citizenry of a city founded in 315 B.C. by a general of Alexander the Great, Cassander, who named it for his wife. In Paul's day it was capital of the Roman province of Macedonia. How many of these christians were Jewish and how many of pagan origin is not known. Statements in the letter indicate that the great majority was from a pagan background.

Paul sees the community as being *'in God the Father and the Lord Jesus Christ.'* This phrase is a distinctively Pauline creation. It transfers the salutation from a banal greeting into the setting for a deep religious communication. Paul announces that he meets them as believers. He deals with them not on a political or social level but in the new world created by God's personal revelation in *'Jesus Christ,'* the act that creates them as a community of believers. God's gifts have transported them from their former sinful state to become sharers of eternal salvation in Jesus.

For Paul the term *'God'* denotes primarily and directly the *'Father'* of Jesus Christ. He is the God who chose Jesus, gave him a mission, raised him from the dead, and now exalts him in glory. Those who accept Jesus' message of life and commit themselves to him with faith receive a new kind of existence. This is what Paul means when he uses the phrase *'in Christ.'* Here he designates this new manner of existence as being in both *'the Father'* and *'Christ.'* God alone can initiate the giving of the new life that makes believers a *'new creation'* (Gal 6:15).

This new life was an extremely vivid experience for Paul who did not look upon it as simply a moral change. Its agent and communicator is *'the Lord Jesus Christ.'* All three nouns of this phrase are important for understanding Paul's meaning. *'Jesus'* is the proper name used by the Son during his earthly existence. *'Christ'* was the title originally used to mark Jesus as the "anointed one," that is, the expected kingly messiah of David's line. Applied to Jesus, Christ soon became accepted as a proper name. This understanding of *Christos* as a personal name is reflected in the practice of simply transliterating it into English as Christ. *'Lord'* is the title Paul uses most often in his letters to identify Jesus as transcending all creation through his resurrection. In glory he now performs the same saving functions that Yahweh performed in Jewish scriptures. Thus, in churches founded by Paul, the characteristic profession of faith was, *'Jesus is Lord'* (cf. 1 Cor 12:3; Phil 2:11). The Septuagint, the Greek translation of the Hebrew Bible, had rendered Yahweh as *kyrios*, Lord. Christians now conferred this title on the risen Jesus.

The composite wish, *'grace to you and peace,'* is a new christian formula of greeting found in all the letters that Paul wrote to churches. It replaces the opening "hail" of secular Greek letters. The term *'grace'* is also found in most of the final closing formulas. In this phrase the verb to be understood is in the optative mood to express a wish. This makes the greeting a blessing or petition formula that God may give its members his favor in Jesus Christ, who is mediator of all the divine benefits believers need to attain eternal life. In the new creation *'in Christ'* everything is *'grace'* because salvation and all the means to obtain it are available as gifts in him alone.

'Peace' is to be understood as translating the Hebrew greeting *shalom*. Like grace it is a gift of God, but carries more concrete connotations. *'Peace'* implies fulness and completion, the total well-being that God's chosen ones confidently expect to enjoy as the ongoing fruits of his fatherly care.

THANKSGIVING FOR THEIR FAITH, LOVE AND HOPE.
1 Thess 1:2-5.

²We give thanks to God always for you all, constantly mentioning you in our prayers, ³remembering before our God and Father your work of faith and labor of love and steadfastness of hope in our Lord Jesus Christ. ⁴For we know, brethren beloved by God, that he has chosen you; ⁵for our gospel came to you not only in word, but also in power and in the Holy Spirit and with full conviction. You know what kind of men we proved to be among you for your sake.

Paul now begins the second part of his letter, technically called the "thanksgiving." This part has been described as a "liturgical telegram," because it focuses on the topic of the letter in the form of a prayer that Paul offers to God in the hearing of the congregation. Its function is to transform the assembly into a worshipping community. The thanksgiving brings them into the dispositions needed to accept the insights and advice that Paul will offer through this letter that Timothy will read to the assembled community. It also filled the practical need of informing the community of the general thrust of the letter. This enabled hearers to be more attentive and to start to motivate their response as they recalled God's favors to them.

In this first of his apostolic letters to various churches Paul prolongs this thanksgiving so that it occupies what is now known as the first two chapters of the letter. This great length manifests Paul's sensitivity both to his own responsibility as an apostle and to the need of preparing this group of immature christians to accept the demands of their new faith. It also shows that Paul is not yet in complete control of the new literary form he is creating but is still groping with it.

'*We give thanks to God.*' Is the thanksgiving a real prayer? Is Paul speaking primarily to God or to the Thessalonians? The truth lies somewhere in the middle. He has turned his attention to their needs with a lively sense of God's presence to him. In the framework of faith Paul exercises the courage and compassion he acquired through personal prayer, but he is actually addressing his converts as their apostle and father in Christ.

The verb '*give thanks*' sets the tone for everything that Paul will say to the assembled group of believers. He shows himself as one deeply involved in their destiny and their difficulties by constantly thinking of all of them. The Greek text is emphatic in expressing the universality of his care, '*always*' for '*all.*' Paul has in mind the divisions present among them and starts to heal them by embracing every member (cf. 4:9-12). The '*God*' he addresses is the Father, as the definite article in Greek makes clear. The Father's loving plan brought them to faith and made them a local church.

Paul specifies in three ways how he thanks God for them. First, '*constantly.*' For his part he can never forget the great favor the Father has bestowed on them and does not want them to forget it either. As their apostle he '*constantly mentions them,*' that is, he lifts them up to the Father in prayer, asking his continued blessings. Toward the end of the letter Paul will recommend to them this same attitude in prayer so that their lives will be God-oriented (5:17).

The second way Paul gives thanks is to spell out God's special gifts to them: '*remembering*' their '*faith . . . love . . . hope.*' These are the three qualities that Paul sees as defining the christian condition (cf. 5:8; 1 Cor 13:13; Gal 5:5-6; Col 1:4-5). In thanking God for bestowing these gifts on this community, Paul is also inviting them to appreciate and cultivate the qualities that later theology will call the "theological virtues," on analogy with the four cardinal virtues of Hellenistic ethics.

The Greek concept of virtue, however, was foreign to Paul's anthropology. He does not look upon faith, love and hope as human achievements; they are effects of God's grace. Paul does not deny the active cooperation of believers with God, for he speaks of *'the work of faith.'* It manifests itself in the changed direction of their lifestyle through the power of their loyalty to Jesus. In later letters Paul calls the attribute in God that evokes faith *'justice'* (cf. Rom 1:17), but here he simply pictures God as the heavenly Father whose care inspires them to total commitment, including obedience to his will (cf. Rom 1:5).

Out of this loyalty and obedience arises the *'labor of love,'* that is, a concern to support one another in their newly chosen life. Very seldom does Paul refer to our love for God. Rather is it God's spirit who pours divine love into believing hearts (cf. Rom 5:5). They then share with one another by this *'labor,'* a word Paul uses below for his missionary labor (2:9; 3:5).

The noun Paul uses for love, *agape*, never appears in any pagan text before New Testament times, although it comes from a verb found as early as Homeric times to denote affectionate concern. *Agape* has none of the romantic connotations of the English word love. Paul speaks of it about 60 times, more than any other New Testament writer. It is the crown and bond of all God's gifts.

Believers exercise this love in the *'steadfastness of hope in our Lord Jesus Christ,'* because their destiny is linked to the victory of Jesus and their striving to share in his glory. The Greek word that describes the *'steadfastness'* of hope includes both the notion of patient endurance, necessary to remain faithful to a christian lifestyle despite opposition, and also certainty of salvation. Christians do not expect the hostile world to accept the path Jesus took. That this small group of believers in Thessalonica has persevered is itself reason to thank God. It is a grace. They manifest themselves as having become an eschatological community, that is, a group that trusts in the death-resurrection of Jesus as inaugurating the final age of salvation. They hope confidently because Jesus has already triumphed and so has banished despair and sadness from their lives (cf. 4:13).

Although it is placed earlier in the English translation, in Greek the phrase *'before our God and Father'* comes after the mention of faith, love and hope. It serves to describe the situation in which Paul imagines himself and the community, namely, in God's presence. They stand together before their loving and concerned Father.

The third manner in which Paul expresses his thanks for them is by an act of knowing. In Greek this verb *'for we know'* is a participle parallel to *'mentioning'* and *'remembering'* above. Paul's recollection of his experience with them is still a powerful motive calling for thanks to God.

He now talks directly to the assembled community, calling them *'brethren, beloved by God.'* This direct address expresses Paul's overpowering sensation of still being present with the church he founded and as an important part of God's gifts to them. He played a crucial role in their new identity as being *'beloved by God.'* This phrase is found on the Rosetta stone of the second century B.C. The word *'beloved'* is a perfect participle in Greek; it designates an ongoing condition resulting from a past action of God. His graciousness toward them in Jesus is the situation out of which flows their new mode of life, and that divine love never ceases. They are permanently *'beloved.'*

This reminder is one way Paul offers encouragement to these young christians who face the difficult challenge of persevering in their new way of life. Implied in Paul's habitual attitude of *'remembering'* is a reminder to them that an attitude of thanks to the Father embraces a willingness to take up their responsibility to cooperate with his saving plan for them.

The sense of being God's chosen people was a belief dear to the Jews. Paul expresses this idea here in Greek by telling them to remember their *'election.'* This term itself never appears in the Hebrew bible. Paul uses it again only in the passage devoted to explaining God's choice of Israel (Rom 9-11). The image still underlies the church's self-understanding of its mission as God's own people.

Paul can make this claim *'for our gospel came to you.'* The term *'gospel'* or good news, used 75 times in the New

Testament including the 54 times Paul uses it in his letters to the churches, became one of the technical terms for the message of salvation available in and through the life, death and resurrection of Jesus. When Paul wrote his letters, the books about the ministry of Jesus that are now called gospels were not yet written. So what does Paul refer to when he uses this term *'gospel'*? Here he means the totality of his witness to his mission on behalf of their salvation (cf. also 2 Thess 2:14). He will enumerate the elements of his witness in the rest of this sentence.

Below he speaks of the *'good news of God'* (2:2) in the sense that the heavenly Father, who is the author of the plan of salvation, has set it in motion by his power and includes them in its fulfilment. In addition to the rhetorical skill that Paul here calls speaking *'only in word,'* he calls attention to manifestations of God's approval of his mission. He displayed oratorical skill but not in the same way as the itinerant philosophical preachers of his day. No; Paul's preaching was a coming *'in power.'* God made his word operative to effect in them a new vision of reality.

In his letters Paul never explicitly refers to performing any miracles. To what then does this *'power'* refer? A similar but expanded phrase appears in Rom 15:19, *'in the power of signs and wonders, in the power of God's spirit.'* Rigaux suggests that this may be a commentary of the shorter expression here. Even so, the exact meaning is not clear to us now. Paul must be thinking of an experience familiar to his readers and so he does not have to make the reference explicit. The Holy Spirit made his *'power'* felt in some striking form during Paul's short stay in Thessalonica. Perhaps this *'power'* was the display of inner strength in Paul through which they could see the Holy Spirit working and overcoming opposition. This presence was a *'power'* that not only sustained Paul but also encouraged them so much that they opened themselves to God's gifts of salvation.

Two factors support this intepretation. First, the absence in Greek of the definite article with *'Holy Spirit,'* so that the phrase could be rendered "in holy-spirit power." In other words, Paul is not speaking of the abstract being of the Holy Spirit but rather of God's sanctifying activity manifest through Paul's apostolic preaching. Second, Paul mentions "holy-spirit joy" in the next verse as being manifest in their lives. They too had a personal experience of the salvation Paul preached as a transcendent *'power'* in their lives (cf. 1 Cor 2:4-5).

The final quality of *'gospel'* that Paul recalls was the *'full conviction'* their conversion brought. They were convinced that God was actively present in their lives. The newness of their experience is reflected in the word itself. This is the first recorded use of the single compound Greek noun translated *'full conviction'*, which appears three more times in the New Testament (Col 2:2; Heb 6:11; 10:22).

Paul next both recapitulates what he has been saying and directs it toward the ethical dimension of the good news in their lives by adding, *'You know what kind of men we proved to be among you for your sake.'* The English translation presents this as an independent statement, but in Greek it is part of the previous sentence and merely adds a further specification to Paul's prayer. Throughout this thanksgiving he prepares the Thessalonians to accept the instructions they need to hear if they are to comply with God's will. By calling attention to the lifestyle of their missionaries Paul suggests that the Holy Spirit enables all believers to live the new life of faith, love and hope, that is, to experience a new dimension of happiness in serving the neighbor and glorifying God.

OPENNESS TO THE GOOD NEWS.
1 Thess 1:6-10.

> [6]And you became imitators of us and of the Lord, for you received the word in much affliction, with joy inspired by the Holy Spirit; [7]so that you became an example to all the believers in Macedonia and in Achaia. [8]For not only has the word of the Lord sounded forth from

you in Macedonia and Achaia, but your faith in God has gone forth everywhere, so that we need not say anything. [9]For they themselves report concerning us what a welcome we had among you, and how you turned to God from idols, to serve a living and true God, [10]and to wait for his Son from heaven, whom he raised from the dead, Jesus who delivers us from the wrath to come.

These verses comprise the concluding part of the opening thanksgiving of the letter. They take the form of a reminder to the community that God's grace has been effective for them. Paul now spells out in fuller detail the work of their faith, love and hope as his motive for thanking God. He also hints at points of misunderstanding that he will have to address later in the letter if he is to help them grow in response to their vocation.

As the apostles who made them into a faith community, Paul and his companions are also the primary models of their response. He rejoices to say, *'you became imitators of us.'* Paul does not appeal to specific incidents in the earthly life of Jesus as models of conduct. Instead, he rejoices to see them imitate the generosity of their first christian teachers, just as he will later rejoice that they imitated the lifestyle of Christian communities in Palestine (2:14). Almost as an afterthought he reminds them that they were also imitators *'of the Lord.'*

How do they imitate the Lord Jesus? As the following phrase shows, Paul is thinking of the earthly Jesus. Just as Jesus' fidelity to his mission brought him opposition, so all who accept God's word must prepare to face affliction and walk the path of bearing his cross. In Paul's eyes the sign that they identify with Jesus is their willingness to submit all their decisions to the inspiration of the Holy Spirit *'with joy.'* He does not appeal to self-motivated psychological satisfaction. This *'joy'* is the deliberately cultivated attitude of embracing their condition as fruit of the Spirit's presence. He led the earthly Jesus; he inspired Paul; now he is with them in *'power.'*

This *'joy'* is *'inspired by the Holy Spirit'* because it
supported them in their *'affliction,'* which is almost a
technical term in Paul for the trials of christians in this final
stage of God's plan, the eschatological period. In Gal 5:22
he lists joy as the fruit of the Spirit second only to love.
It is a special presence of the Spirit enabling believers to
stand in opposition to this world's agenda. Acts of the
Apostles also sees it as a sign of the apostles' fidelity to
their role as proclaimers of the good news (Acts 13:52).

Paul now calls the gospel *'the word.'* This is one of several
New Testament ways to designate God's revelation of
salvation in Jesus. At times Paul expands it to *'word of
God'* (2:13) in that it communicates the Father's plan, or to
'word of the Lord' (1:8; cf. 2 Thess 3:1), for he is the fulfill-
ment of God's good news, as noted above. When the gospel
is *'received,'* like the seed of the parable, into willing souls,
it produces fruitfulness.

Their imitation of Paul and of the fidelity of Jesus to the
cross has already made them so fruitful that they are a model
of conduct for the newly founded communities in the whole
area of modern Greece and Albania, *'so that you became
an example.'* This statement is a testimony to the vitality
of the Thessalonian community. Within the few months
since Paul left, they have already become known for loyalty
to their new faith. From what follows Paul is evidently
speaking about a missionary outreach. The term used here
to designate the Thessalonians as *'believers'* is the Greek
participle that never became a common title in the New
Testament, although it has become a common way to
identify them later in history.

In 1:8-10 Paul reports the impact they made on christian
communities of the area in two ways, namely: (1) by *'sending
forth'* the message of the good news, here called *'the word
of the Lord,'* that is, the message of salvation as a gift in the
Lord Jesus, who is the subject of what they believe; (2) by
the witness of their loyalty toward God. By contrast, Paul
will accuse Jews of trying to prevent apostles from sharing

the message of salvation (2:16). In this ongoing tension Paul will pray that the word may speed and become triumphant (2 Thess 3:1). In the original text Paul changes his direction in the middle of verse 8, thus creating an anacoluthon, or shift of grammatical construction within the sentence. This grammatical inconsistency, a mark of emotion or oral style, has been smoothed over in the RSV translation.

The tone of these verses gives the impression that Paul is completely satisfied with the community—an impression that will change later. To create positive feelings of self-acceptance within the community is part of the role of the opening thanksgiving of the letter. Paul uses this approach to encourage the young community and to open them to hear instructions that will make demands upon them. Verse 9 provides the basis for this method. Paul reminds the Thessalonians that believing is a fundamental choice, a choice that implies their willingness to embrace the whole christian commitment.

In stating what those communities *'report,'* Paul refers to three specific events: (1) his warm reception by those who became believers in Thessalonica. Right from the beginning their response was total. This openness is the quality that Paul will rely upon later in this letter to encourage their perseverence. (2) The members of this community were originally pagan, although the account in Acts 17:1 shows that at least some were converts from Judaism. All of them undertook a change of lifestyle when they embraced this new belief. The phrase *'living God'* is rare in the Hebrew bible but appears 15 times in the New Testament. Only here does Paul call God *'true,'* a title that is common in John. Here it means the real God in contrast to idols. The God whom Paul preaches promises unending life to believers, but he also makes demands upon them.

(3) The third event that was widely reported as confirmation of the Thessalonians' faith in the *'living and true God'* was their apocalyptic hope, described in verse 10. Their

conversion brought all their activity under the saving influence of *'his Son,'* the risen Christ who is actively present to his followers. This form of hope, which is characteristic of christian faith, formed the climax of Paul's remembrance above (1:3).

Paul now specifies their hope as he attributes salvation directly to the coming of Jesus as God's glorious *'Son from heaven.'* Paul is evidently alluding to the apocalyptic figure of the Book of Daniel, the *'Son of Man,'* although he never uses this term in his letters. Jesus will display his prerogatives when he comes as universal judge in favor of his people. He will vindicate those who believe that God has *'raised'* him from among *'the dead.'* This is the only time that Paul describes christian hope as *'waiting for'* Jesus. In his later letters he uses terms that convey a more interior receptivity.

Paul will now go on to expand these three descriptions of the Thessalonians' response to God's grace as a way of encouraging them to persevere in their christian vocation. Only after that will he outline specific directions on how they are to act in the future (cf. 3:9-5:22). He refers again to the apocalyptic *'wrath to come'* in 5:9.

PAUL'S EXPERIENCE AMONG THEM.
1 Thess 2:1-8.

> **2** For you yourselves know, brethren, that our visit to you was not in vain; [2]but though we had already suffered and been shamefully treated at Philippi, as you know, we had courage in our God to declare to you the gospel of God in the face of great opposition. [3]For our appeal does not spring from error or uncleanness, nor is it made with guile; [4]but just as we have been approved by God to be entrusted with the gospel, so we speak, not to please men, but to please God who tests our hearts. [5]For we never used either words of flattery, as you know, or a cloak for greed, as God is witness; [6]nor did we seek glory

from men, whether from you or from others, though we might have made demands as apostles of Christ. [7]But we were gentle[a] among you, like a nurse taking care of her children. [8]So, being affectionately desirous of you, we were ready to share with you not only the gospel of God but also our own selves, because you had become very dear to us.

[a]Other ancient authorities read *babes.*

Chapter 2 of this letter provides Paul's most complete description of evangelizing a pagan community. The first two parts (2:1-8 and 9-12) develop the allusion in the thanksgiving (1:5) to the type of persons who evangelized them. These descriptions prepare for a feature of the letter called the "apostolic parousia," in which Paul voices his desire to join them again. Since he cannot fulfill this desire in person at present, he substitutes this letter for his personal presence (*parousia*).

Paul elaborates what kind of persons he and his fellow evangelists are in the form of four "disclosures" of their apostolic activity (2:1-4, 5-8, 9-10, 11-12). These are followed by a second thanksgiving prayer to God for the receptivity of the Thessalonian community to the gospel (2:13-16). Paul's vocabulary and style are so much like that of contemporary Cynic orations in this section that it is not clear whether he is referring to actual events in his own ministry or merely using rhetorical commonplaces to emphasize his concern.

First disclosure (2:1-4): Paul's sincerity. He introduces this outpouring of affection by addressing the community as *'brethren,'* the title found 14 times in this letter. He repeats this word from the thanksgiving (1:4), as well as the belief that God has chosen them. Here, however, he does so in the form of understatement or litotes by saying that his preaching was *'not in vain,'* meaning that it proved a channel of God's grace for them. They enjoyed and responded to God's manifest power.

The experience of a fruitful harvest came as a consolation to Paul after the painful experience of being rejected and expelled from Philippi. The compound verb translated here as *'already suffered'* appears nowhere else in scripture. Why does Paul mention this treatment? It serves as a mark of authenticity for him as a christian preacher and apostle. Disciples of Jesus always suffer from hostility from unbelievers. Their ability to overcome this opposition in proclaiming the good news comes from divine power. Thus the community saw Paul, Silvanus and Timothy as revealers of the *'gospel of God,'* that is, as making available the Father's plan to save all who commit themselves to Jesus.

Continued opposition made Paul conscious of the impact being made by all kinds of itinerant preachers motivated by a variety of goals. Ironically using the style of a Cynic philosopher, Paul contrasts himself with those preachers to proclaim that his exhortation is not animated by: (1) *'error'*—a false concept of God that fostered idolatry and other sins of pagans; (2) *'uncleanness'*—deceitful motivation to lead them astray, or (3) *'guile'*—taking advantage of them to trick them by a false message.

Paul rounds out this first disclosure with a comprehensive positive statement of his God-given mission and his fidelity to it. This balance of negative and positive expressions will appear again in the following disclosure (2:5-8). From this point Paul moves into a general apologia for his apostolic team. Paul represents their mission as having been carried out with divine approval. He repeats the verb *'approved'* at the end of the sentence, but there it is translated as *'tests.'* The same verb appears in 1 Pt 1:7 of gold *'tested by fire.'* Implied in this statement is that Paul's fidelity to God's grace is the model for their response to their call.

The *'so'* of the RSV is not to be understood as stating result but as conveying the manner of Paul's proclaiming the gospel, namely, exactly as God wanted him to do. The description of God as the one *'who tests our hearts'* is modeled on the confessions of Jeremiah (Jer 11:20), to whom Paul at times compared himself. In biblical terminology *'heart'* has a wide range of significance; it was considered the seat of both insight and judgment.

Second disclosure (2:5-8): Paul's integrity. This passage is also introduced by the conjunction *'for.'* It is cast in the same pattern as the first disclosure: three denials of wrongdoing plus a positive explanation of Paul's conduct. The three courses of action that he rejected were:

(1) using words of *'flattery.'* The philosopher Philodemus of the first century B.C. wrote a tract on flattery, but the word never appears elsewhere in the bible. The added phrase *'as you know'* implies that Paul is responding to real accusations against himself and his fellow missionaries.

(2) using preaching as *'a cloak for greed.'* They did not offer their message under false colors to distract from personal greed—*'God is witness.'* In Paul's time itinerant preachers worked for a fee. Perhaps that is why he insisted on earning his own living. He saw that choice as a proof of his integrity.

(3) We did not *'seek glory from men.'* In itself this phrase is open to a wide range of interpretation. What Paul had in mind is seen from the specification, *'though we might have made demands as apostles of Christ.'* Paul and his companions could have demanded support in accordance with the Lord's instruction that his disciples should be supported by those receiving the good news. By telling his disciples not to carry bread or coins, Jesus entrusted them to the care of believers (cf. Mk 6:8). This command was close to Paul's heart and he reflects upon it later in 1 Cor 9:4-18. Crucial for understanding Paul's self-defense here is his use of the title *'apostles of Christ'*—the only time he uses it in the Thessalonian correspondence. Some New Testament authors limit this title to the close personal companions of the earthly Jesus commissioned by him to continue his missions. Paul's extension of the term *'apostle'* may have been influenced by the Cynic use of this title for their wise men.

The positive side of this second disclosure comes in verses 7-8. Paul describes his conduct as *'gentle among you, like a nurse taking care of her children.'* This image is a commonplace in Hellenistic philosphy. Instead of *'gentle,'* some ancient manuscripts read that the apostles were *'babes.'* That reading results from doubling a single Greek letter, but it is to be rejected as out of context with the expansion in the following sentence that begins, *'So, being affectionately desirous.'* This long English phrase is needed to translate the participle of a single Greek verb that appears only here in the New Testament.

Paul describes his apostolic mission by using the figure of a devoted nurse toward her *own* children. The Greek text has the reflexive pronoun that is not translated in the RSV. Why doesn't he simply say mother? If we remember that exposure of infants was extremely common in his time, mere mention of the term mother would not communicate the depth of devotion Paul wants to convey. In addition, *'nurse'* conveys the subordinate role that preachers play in relation to the divine grace they receive and share.

Deep affection was the hallmark of Paul's life as an apostle. He was eager to imitate Jesus in handing his life over for them out of love because they were *'very dear'* *(agapetoi)* to him. This Greek adjective comes from the common New Testament word for love *(agape)* that designates neither sexual love *(eros)* nor family love *(philia)*. Christian *agape* is a deliberate, carefully cultivated unselfish concern for others that imitates God's saving concern in sending Jesus as savior. Paul attributes this love to his companions as well as himself. But their willingness to share of themselves is not presented as an act of expiation as was the death of Jesus, *'for us.'* It was rather an act of service to carry on Christ's work and to make it available to others. St. John Chrysostom uses these verses as the basis for a paean of Christian friendship.

THE POWER OF APOSTOLIC EXAMPLE.
1 Thess 2:9-12.

> [9]For you remember our labor and toil, brethren; we worked night and day, that we might not burden any of you, while we preached to you the gospel of God. [10]You are witnesses, and God also, how holy and righteous and blameless was our behavior to you believers; [11]for you know how, like a father with his children, we exhorted each one of you and encouraged you and charged you [12]to lead a life worthy of God, who calls you into his own kingdom and glory.

Paul continues to reflect on his experience in relation to them by making his third disclosure (2:9-10): apostolic unselfishness. His aim in adopting this style of writing is to encourage them. He is still preparing them for the demands that their christian vocation makes. He mentions the generous response he and his companions gave to preaching at Thessalonica, *'You remember our labor and toil.'* Again he addresses them as *'brethren,'* a reminder that they have been raised to the same new relationship to God through faith in Jesus.

Paul encourages them to think about how their missionaries had conducted themselves there, namely, by assuming the extra burden of supporting themselves so that their preaching would not put another burden upon the community. He makes explicit what he implied in the second disclosure (2:6)—he preached at his own expense. The word Paul uses for preach means literally *'to proclaim like a herald.'* This verb is found 16 times in Paul's letters to the churches, either absolutely, or followed by the complement *'gospel'* or *'Christ.'* In modern times the corresponding noun *'kerygma'* has been employed by religious educators to designate the content of early Christian preaching as summarized in the speeches in Acts.

Paul is thus continuing to contrast the conduct of Silvanus, Timothy and himself with the grasping lifestyle of itinerant philosophical preachers. Christian preaching is an example of what Paul called *'the work of faith'* in the opening thanksgiving (1:3). It demands serious and unselfish *'labor and toil.'* The term *'toil'* specifies the preaching apostolate as a difficult and demanding responsibility.

Paul links three adverbs to summarize this apostolic style of conduct. They come out in the RSV text as adjectives, *'holy and righteous and blameless.'* In addition to the stylistic feature of using groups of three, the phrase serves as testimony to the transforming power of the good news because these three abstracts cover the areas of relationships with God and with neighbor as well as personal integrity. Toward the end of this letter (5:23), Paul will pray that they may also live blamelessly. Such repetitions and reinforcements alert readers to the fact that Paul had an agenda in mind as he wrote and that a unity of vision underlies the unfolding of his letters.

Fourth disclosure (2:11-12): Paul's fatherly concern. Paul's growing emotional intensity reflects itself in the irregular style. First, he omits the verb in comparing himself to a father; then he continues by switching to participles. This emotion is hidden by their being translated into English as finite verbs. Paul brings his long series of reflections to a close by comparing the team's service to a father's acts of exhorting, encouraging (cf. 5:14) and insisting. The meaning of these three verbs is not clearly distinct but the combination testifies to Paul's deep concern that the Thessalonians will respond to God's call to his *'kingdom.'* The use of the *'kingdom'* image is not frequent in Paul (cf. Rom 14:17; 1 Cor 4:20; 15:50; Col 4:11).

Paul's purpose in prolonging this part of the letter is his pastoral sense that he must make them more receptive to the warnings and moral directives he will have to give later. Just as God's grace has changed the lives of their preachers so it gives them the ability to alter their lifestyle and to proclaim their new faith with courage. Ultimately the strongest religious motivation is simply to narrate the great blessings that make believers sharers of God's *'own kingdom and glory.'* The term *'glory'* is the biblical way of designating a public display of God's saving power to transform persons.

God's *'glory'* will be manifest in their leading *'a life worthy of God.'* In Greek this phrase is expressed in the image of walking, a figure common in both Greek and biblical literature to designate conduct of life. It is one of Paul's favorite images (cf. below 4:1,12; Rom 6:4; 1 Cor 3:3; 2 Cor 5:7). In fact, this whole series of four disclosures reveals an imaginative and pastoral side of Paul's personality that is often neglected in commentaries or misunderstood by those who stress only his doctrinal thrust. Here we can see why St. John Chrysostom, ardent admirer and brilliant commentator of Paul, said, "The heart of Paul is the heart of Christ."

THEIR LOYALTY IN SPITE OF OPPOSITION.
1 Thess 2:13-16.

> [13]And we also thank God constantly for this, that when you received the word of God which you heard from us, you accepted it not as the word of men but as what it really is, the word of God, which is at work in you believers. [14]For you, brethren, became imitators of the churches of God in Christ Jesus which are in Judea; for you suffered the same things from your own countrymen as they did from the Jews, [15]who killed both the Lord Jesus and the prophets, and drove us out, and displease God and oppose all men [16]by hindering us from speaking to the Gentiles that they may be saved—so as always to fill up the measure of their sins. But God's wrath has come upon them at last![b]

[b]Or *completely,* or *for ever.*

Several recent commentators have called into question the authenticity of this paragraph because of both its form and content. As to form, it is a thanksgiving. As mentioned above, the thanksgiving is ordinarily found at the beginning of Paul's letters, immediately following the address (cf. 1:2-10). If this paragraph were not present, this letter would follow the expected movement of a Pauline letter. In fact, this second thanksgiving disturbs the natural flow of thought between the series of recollections or disclosures (2:1-12) and Paul's expression of a desire to see them, the so-called "apostolic parousia," found in the next paragraph (2:17-20).

As to content, this second thanksgiving expresses a harshness towards the Jews never found elsewhere in Paul's letters. He goes out of his way to say that they *'killed'* Jesus and the prophets and that they *'displease God.'* Furthermore, this is the only passage in the early New Testament writings stating that the Jews in Judea persecuted the christians. Commentators opposed to its authenticity say that these statements reflect a period after 70 A.D. when Jewish christians were being excommunicated from synagogues and hostility between Jews and christians was increasing. These tensions are evident in Acts of the Apostles.

On the other hand, this new thanksgiving relates well to the situation Paul has just reflected upon. Such personal recollections could easily erupt into the new prayer with its allusions to the source of tensions in this young community. That would explain why he repeats several words and phrases from his opening thanksgiving (cf. 1:2-6); and yet Paul turns to a special motive for thanking God, namely, the way they received *'the word of God.'* The Thessalonians received the preaching precisely as a gift of God and not as the product of any human wisdom. They could do so only because God's *'word'* was *'at work'* in them to make them believers. All biblical manuscripts contain this passage. Formal arguments against it are not sufficient to eliminate it because Paul is still working out the form of an apostolic letter.

In this thanksgiving Paul jams into one long sentence a whole series of events to remind the hearers of how much God has done for them. His prayer serves as an added incentive for undertaking the new lifestyle that Paul will later lay out for them. They do not have to fear because God's *'word'* is actively *'at work'* in and among them. Because they *'accepted'* it with faith, the Thessalonians experienced its transforming power in themselves. Paul expresses the biblical notion of the creative power of God's word, which in the New Testament is treated much like personified wisdom in the Hebrew bible. In John's gospel it will become a title for the Son of God incarnate in Jesus Christ.

Once again Paul maintains the atmosphere of his personal presence and of their equality before God by addressing them as *'brethren.'* Modifying a phrase from the opening thanksgiving, he praises them because they *'became imitators of the churches of God in Christ Jesus which are in Judea.'* The stress is on being *'in Christ Jesus,'* Paul's often repeated theological phrase (cf. on 1:1) that summarizes their new relationship to God accomplished by the saving mission of Jesus, Lord of the new covenant. Belief is a journey into Christ.

Acts of the Apostles mentions activities of Jews in Palestine against christians living *'in Judea'* soon after the resurrection of Jesus (cf. 8:1-4; involving Paul in 9:1-2; led by Herod in 12:1-4). Paul talks about his own former attacks on christians in Gal 1:13 and Phil 3:6. But it is not clear why Paul should hold up Jews in Judea as prototypes of the Thessalonians' *'own countrymen'* who were inflicting suffering on them. Perhaps he is venting personal anger at the conduct of Corinthian Jews toward him at the moment of his writing. In any case, Paul does not repeat this kind of outburst in later letters unless 2 Thess 3:2 alludes to the same situation. By contrast, he displays a highly sympathetic attitude toward Jews in Rom 9:3-5.

Paul's emotion is reflected in the complicated syntax of the long and intricate sentence structure of this second thanksgiving. Yet it does not prevent him from an artistic use of participles. He uses them to present four charges against the Jews. Of these the first two are in the past: (1) that they killed the prophets and Jesus (cf. Mt 23:34,37; compare Rom 11:3, which quotes 1 Kgs 19:10 attributing a similar charge to Elijah), and (2) that they persecuted Paul and his companions. The last two charges are ongoing: (3) Jews are displeasing to God, and (4) they are opposed to the salvation of pagans.

This outburst is hard to explain because it is directed against Jews rather than against those who are in the actual opponents of the Thessalonians. Paul presents the Jews as suffering for the offenses mentioned above by experiencing the divine anger, *'God's wrath,'* called the *'wrath to come'* in 1:10. Paul states their punishment in the apocalyptic imagery familiar to Jews of his time and appropriate for his own vivid expectation of Christ's return in glory.

In this context Paul gives a crisp summary of the apostolic role in the divine plan. It consists of three elements:

(1) *'to speak.'* Apostles are chosen to proclaim the good news of salvation not simply in fleeting words but as heralds of salvation by their whole manner of life and total commitment to God's revelation (cf. v. 2 above). Their message belongs to the class of speech that J. L. Austin termed "performative." It was a speaking that did something: judged and saved, enlightened and converted (cf. 1:5; 2:13).

(2) *'to the Gentiles.'* Literally in Greek, *'to the nations,'* which was the Jewish term for pagans. Later Paul will speak of himself as one chosen by God to preach the good news to the Gentiles (Gal 1:16). This does not mean that the Jews are excluded from salvation. In fact, in his preaching Paul went first to synagogues to invite Jews to believe. Only when his efforts met with rejection did he devote himself to the salvation of the pagans. At this earlier stage in his apostolic career Paul is asserting that all are called by God to salvation. His missionary approach was accepted by the Jerusalem community in their meeting with him (cf. Acts 15). Later Paul developed a theological interpretation of the widespread refusal of Jews to believe in Jesus (Rom 9-11).

(3) *'that they may be saved.'* Paul states in another way the pure motivation of christian preachers in contrast to the self-seeking of itinerant Cynic preachers. The apostles act as agents of God who alone can save. He sent them to deliver humanity from the slavery of sin and the power of the evil one. Their mission provokes a crisis of conscience and demands acceptance or rejection. Because the preaching of the gospel demands choice, this phrase reminds the believing community of their responsibility to continue to respond to God's grace.

PAUL WANTS TO SEE THEM.
1 Thess 2:17-20.

> [17]But since we were bereft to you, brethren, for a short time, in person not in heart, we endeavored the more eagerly and with great desire to see you face to face; [18]because we wanted to come to you—I, Paul, again and again—but Satan hindered us. [19]For what is our hope or joy or crown of boasting before our Lord Jesus at his coming? Is it not you? [20]For you are our glory and joy.

This is the first paragraph of a new section that commentators who study the structure of Paul's letters call the "apostolic parousia" (2:17-3:10). In this section Paul points to his use of letter writing as a temporary substitute for personal presence and promises to visit them in his capacity as their apostle. He is forced to resort to writing because a visit with them is impossible at the moment.

In his concern for their welfare Paul had sent Timothy to find out their situation first hand. Timothy's report raised serious problems, but Paul sees that he will be unable to visit them in the near future. This letter is his follow-up on the report to lay down a mode of conduct for them until he can come. But before getting into specific details of what they are to do (cf. 3:10-5:22), Paul "visits" with them in this outpouring of personal affection and appreciation, introduced by addressing them once more as *'brethren.'*

His expression, *'we were bereft of you,'* occurs nowhere else in the bible. Literally it means "made an orphan" and is a strong image for Paul's love for the Thessalonians. It is replaced by his absent-in-body-present-in-mind image in 1 Cor 5:3 and Col 2:5. He refers to this condition as existing *'for a short time.'* The RSV chooses this interpretation, but the Greek phrase can also mean "at present." In either case the separation provides Paul with the occasion to voice his *'great desire to see you face to face.'*

His motive is affectionate concern, *'because we wanted to come to you—I, Paul, again and again.'* By switching from his usual plural to the singular Paul specifies the desire as personal. Yet he returns to the plural in the same sentence, *'but Satan hindered us.'* This stated cause for Paul's frustration shows the gap between our modern sense of contingent causality and his apocalyptic mindset. Today we could think of Paul's pressing apostolic commitments at Corinth as preventing a visit to them. Exactly what interference he speaks of is not clear—perhaps satanic influence behind resistance to evangelization. Satan is said to be the cause behind Judas' betrayal of Jesus (Lk 22:3; Jn 13:2,27). Paul could also be alluding to some personal situation such as sickness, conceived by him as brought on by Satan (cf. 2 Cor 12:7). This could have been serious enough to prevent a visit by Silvanus, Timothy and Paul. He attributed such events to Satan as prince of this world with real power in the physical realm.

Paul can endure these trials because his ultimate *'hope'* is everlasting reunion with the community at the last judgment when all will stand *'before our Lord Jesus at his coming.'* The Greek word for *'coming' (parousia)* became a technical term in the apostolic church for the glorious return of the risen Jesus as judge of the living and the dead (cf. 1 Thess 3:13; 4:15; 5:23; 2 Thess 2:1; Mt 24:27,37,39; 1 Cor 15:23; 2 Pt 3:4). Paul's choice of two rhetorical questions, *"What is our hope . . . Is it not you?'* to voice this hope is his way of showing his confidence in their loyalty even when he cannot be with them.

Paul sees his own faithful apostolic service in preaching and setting up communities of faith as the basis for his own *'boasting'* at the final judgment. They will be his *'crown of boasting.'* Here Paul combines two images that he uses separately in prayer elsewhere. The community at Philippi is his *'joy and crown'* (Phil 4:1), appearing also in an apocalyptic text. Paul also prayed that members of the church at Philippi would conduct themselves blamelessly and thus be his *'boast'* on the day of the Lord's judgment (Phil 2:16). And he prayed that the Corinthian community would come to know him better so that they would be each other's *'boast'* on the day of the Lord (2 Cor 1:14).

His whole career as an apostle was God's gift to them. Since Paul relied not on natural talents or rhetorical stratagems but solely upon the working of God's grace that brings both preacher and those evangelized into the fulness of life, he treated them as his *'glory and joy.'* In biblical language the term *'glory' (doxa)* designates the external display of power—primarily God's (cf. 2:12). When it refers to humans, it signifies renown or reputation or honor (cf. 2:6). Here Paul means that their good example has enhanced the team's reputation as apostles. He wishes to maintain that renown, and this desire has led him to continue to foster contact with them. He did so by means of the mission of Timothy that he will now recall as the transition into the advice his report calls forth.

WHY PAUL IS SENDING TIMOTHY AGAIN.
1 Thess 3:1-5.

> **3** Therefore when we could bear it no longer, we were willing to be left behind at Athens alone, [2]and we sent Timothy, our brother and God's servant in the gospel of Christ, to establish you in your faith and to exhort you, [3]that no one be moved by these afflictions. You yourselves know that this is to be our lot. [4]For when we

were with you, we told you beforehand that we were to suffer affliction; just as it has come to pass, and as you know. ⁵For this reason, when I could bear it no longer, I sent that I might know your faith, for fear that somehow the tempter had tempted you and that our labor would be in vain.

This paragraph about the sending of Timothy is not only written in a tight unity but plays an important role in leading up to the paragraph that will present Paul's specific instructions to the church at Thessalonica. The amount of time and skill that Paul extends to lay the groundwork for his instruction calls forth serious consideration on the part of modern readers. How Paul functions as an apostle of this community tells us much about how he conceives his mission. His care to prepare them to hear his concern shows that the task of expanding horizons is an integral part of transmitting a message, because sender and receiver must be in the same world.

Paul's anxiety about their growth in their new faith prompted him to send Timothy to see how they were weathering the trials that followers of Jesus Christ are bound to experience. The background of this letter is found in Acts of the Apostles 17:1-16, but details of these two writings do not mesh. Timothy is not mentioned in the account in Acts of the visit of Paul and Silas (Silvanus) to Thessalonica. While other Christians took Paul to Athens, Timothy and Silas remained at Beroea. Paul gave orders that they were to join him at Athens as soon as possible.

Acts implies a short stay in Athens for Paul because he failed to attract converts. He went on to Corinth, and Silas and Timothy joined him there (Acts 18:5). Thus Acts omits any mention of Timothy's mission in Thessalonica. Why? Each literary production has its own aim. No New Testament writing is concerned primarily with providing a mere chronicle of external events. What Paul does in this letter is to reaffirm his fatherly affection for the Thessalonians.

His anxiety for their growth in faith was so great that he could *'bear'* it no longer—a verb he uses at both the beginning and end of this paragraph as a literary "inclusion" (3:1,5). Inclusion is the rhetorical figure of repeating a word from the beginning of a section at the end in order to set it off as a unit. Because of his short stay with them, Paul did not have a chance to come to know the new converts at Thessalonica intimately or to complete his instructions about the christian life.

Now he must give them advice that will make demands on their way of living. He spends a large part of the letter preparing the soil of their hearts with great care so that his words will be accepted and bear fruit. Paul is the only biblical writer to use the idiom about *'bearing'* up in a difficult situation (cf. 1 Cor 9:12; 13:7). His anxiety made him *'willing'* to send Timothy there as his representative although it meant that he had to remain *'at Athens alone.'* Paul used the same verb *'willing'* earlier to express his desire to share the good news with them (2:8). His use of the plural thoughout this passage is a carry-over from the letter-writing style, for he is talking about his individual feelings toward them.

In the RSV text Paul describes Timothy as *'our brother and God's servant in the gospel of Christ.'* Great discrepancy exists in the manuscript readings at this point, but the original title given to Timothy seems to have been God's *'fellow worker'* rather than *'servant'*. Paul frequently refers to others as his fellow workers, but only in 1 Cor 3:9 does he speak of evangelizers as *'God's fellow workers.'* The boldness of using this title for Timothy here evidently led copyists to modify the expression. The result is the variety of readings found in the manuscripts. Yet this bold praise of Timothy fits Paul's purpose of raising the morale of the Thessalonian christians who have been favored to hear the good news that Jesus Christ is their Savior.

The effect of the visit of Timothy in their regard was twofold: to solidify them in their *'faith'* and to *'exhort'* them so that their *'afflictions'* would not shake them. The Greek text indicates that these were not two separate actions but two dimensions of a single dynamic. That is, by making them more firm in their confidence in God, Timothy encouraged them to persevere; and by encouraging them, he gave them deeper insight to remain faithful to the message of the good news. From both angles his mission shored them up against being *'moved'* by the hostility brought on through their loyalty to living their faith. The English *'moved'* is a weak translation of a verb that never appears elsewhere in the bible. It means to be shaken or disturbed and seduced from their commitment.

In his opening thanksgiving prayer Paul reminded them that *'affliction'* is part of living out the good news (1:6; cf. 2:14), and that it remains an ongoing element of christian life. Paul repeats this truth strongly in this paragraph: trials are the *'lot'* of believers. He says this with emphasis by repeating the verb *'know'* in verses 3 and 4. This knowing is not so much intellectual as experiential, as the special conjunction connecting these two verses indicates. It is the idiomatic Greek particle *kai gar*, a phrase found 20 times in Paul's letters, most often in his Corinthian correspondence. It is limited to hortatory passages (cf. 4:10, reworked in 2 Thess 3:10).

As here in the RSV, *kai gar* is ordinarily translated *'for,'* but that is an inaccurate and misleading translation because it does not introduce a logical reason. Rather it intensifies awareness or emotion. This conjunction is a good example of what linguists call phatic communication. The phatic dimension of communication is to keep channels open. It is as though Paul bursts forth in a gentle chiding tone, "I told you so! How could you forget?" Paul is expressing his apocalyptic view of the world scene; it is the final age and its *'afflictions'* are the birthpangs of the reign of God. That is why they are the *'lot'* of christians, citizens of the new age. It seems as if Paul is saying that christians exist to be persecuted (cf. Acts 14:22). From their own personal experience the Thessalonians now really *'know'* what Paul had told them.

He closes this paragraph by returning to his opening expression of concern, he *'could bear it no longer,'* but now he writes in the first person singular. His own need to know that they were persevering in *'faith'* despite all obstacles was the real impetus for sending Timothy. This is the second time Paul speaks of faith in this paragraph and he will mention it twice in the next paragraph (3:6,7). His repeated emphasis on faith as the foundation of christian existence reveals the lasting impact of his own conversion experience. Jesus taught him that salvation is a free gift on God's part creating a new dimension of human existence. Grace makes faith possible and free. By the response of faith all believers become equally children of God; there are no second-class christians. Paul wants to make sure that the Thessalonian christians value their new *'lot.'*

Only this vivid appreciation of their divine gift is strong enough to keep them alert against *'the tempter,'* a title used in the New Testament only here and in Mt 4:3. The ordinary title for the devil, found over 30 times in its writings, is Satan (cf. 2:18). The Lord's prayer in Matthew's version prays that we may not succumb to the temptation that is linked to the final apocalyptic battle (Mt 6:13). Constant awareness of the cleverness of Satan helps us to be on guard against falling prey to his treachery. The last two phrases of this paragraph express complementary concerns of Paul: 1) his fear that Satan had *'tempted'* them—a possibility that disturbed him; 2) his fear that their apostles' *'labor would be in vain'*—still a future possibility.

Earlier Paul told them that his missionary coming had not been *'in vain'* (2:1). Now his concern is to make sure they will not lose out at the final judgment lest his work for them be *'in vain.'* The whole tenor of this paragraph is calculated to strengthen the self-image of the community members and protect them from feeling isolated. Paul's extended conversation with them about past relationships is another important step in laying the groundwork for the demands he is going to make upon the faith he has been praising. Their awareness of how much he esteems them will be a powerful incentive to confirm Paul's *'labor.'* We may assume that the complement *'of love'* is to be understood with *'labor,'* as in 1:3. Mutual christian love exercised in the *'patience of hope'* (1:3) is a necessary sign of true faith.

PAUL REJOICES AT TIMOTHY'S REPORT.
1 Thess 3:6-8.

> [6]But now that Timothy has come to us from you, and has brought us the good news of your faith and love and reported that you always remember us kindly and long to see us, as we long to see you—[7]for this reason, brethren, in all our distress and affliction we have been comforted about you through your faith; [8]for now we live, if you stand fast in the Lord.

Paul abruptly changes the time of events he is discussing and switches to the time after Timothy's return. But he still does not state the problems facing the community. Rather he first reports in joyful language the glowing account of Timothy and the encouragement he received from it. In the Greek text this section is all one sentence that contains an anacoluthon. This is, Paul changes direction at the beginning of verse 7. This is indicated in the RSV translation by a dash.

The opening phrase *'now that'* indicates that Paul wrote soon after the return of Timothy. He considered this an important report that needed to be acted upon promptly so that the community would move in a fruitful direction. The verb Paul uses to describe Timothy's report, *'brought us the good news,'* is a single word in Greek, the word that became a technical term for communicating the message of salvation through Jesus the Messiah. This is the only time in Paul's letters that the term keeps its general sense of giving a report that people are happy to hear. This appearance is a reminder that christian technical vocabulary came from the application of words in common language to a special context. The words kept their wider range of meaning that could still be utilized by writers and speakers. In communication words do not have meaning apart from their context, and always interact with it.

The report of Timothy embraced three items: the Thessalonians' *'faith,'* their *'love'* and their fond recollection of Paul. These were the concerns that Paul spoke of above. He keeps the primacy of faith before their eyes so that they will not think they can achieve their destiny by breaking away from the new reality they share only if they *'stand fast in the Lord.'* Believers must continue to evaluate all that happens in terms of their call to be in Christ. They have a test for the loyalty of faith, namely, the fervor of *'love'* in the sense of their active concern for one another in Christ (cf. 1:3), and by their thanksgiving for the gifts he gives. The life that the faithful now *'live'* is creative concern for one another *'in the Lord.'* Paul is putting the final touches on his long process of orienting them to hear the advice he is now about to begin. It will center on how they are to exercise the *'faith'* and *'love'* Timothy praised in them.

Paul singles out a third element in the report: they cherish fond memories of Paul and *'long to see'* him with much the same intensity that he expressed to see them (2:17). For Paul, christian life deepens its roots by fostering mutual presence and support, a characteristic that he will often express in the image of building up one another—found for the first time in this letter (5:11). Paul placed great importance on that form of love because he saw that the small christian communities were open to various forms of harrassment for their loyalty to Christ.

Paul suddenly breaks off these reflections and concludes them with a word of thanks to the community as *'brethren,'* telling them how much their strong faith has *'comforted'* him in all his *'distress and affliction.'* He refers to his recent disappointments, alluding no doubt to his rejection at Athens, along with continued opposition from his own people. By this choice of words Paul identifies himself as one who is undergoing eschatological *'affliction'* related to the new age (cf. 1:6).

He ends this transitional passage with another expression of gratitude to them and a plea for their perseverance: *'for we live if you stand fast in the Lord.'* Just how does the faith and perseverance of the Thessalonians contribute to Paul's ability to *'live'?* It is tempting simply to pass over this phrase as hyperbolic language. But it goes deeper than that. This protestation demands a serious look at the personality of Paul and his deep involvement as apostle in the growth of the communities he formed. His role went far beyond a communication of information. It was a sharing in a new world on every level. The very act of undertaking to write this letter must have stirred Paul to a more profound awareness of God's choice of him as an apostle. He has a significant part to play in bringing about the transformation that Christ's redemption creates for humanity.

By such a personal outpouring Paul reminded the Thessalonians of their privileged role *'in the Lord'* before asking them to intensify their response to the good news. In a real way the continued faith of believing communities *'comforted'* the spirit of Paul and was part of the grace of his apostolate. Passages like this provided occasion for patristic commentators to reflect on the spirituality of Paul, as B. Rigaux indicates by giving a few select quotations.

This is the context in which Paul coins the almost untranslatable expression *'in the Lord'* that appears so often in his letters. It is an abbreviated way of summarizing the whole new form of existence available only through faith in Jesus Christ. The frequency with which it flows from Paul's lips bears witness to its central place in his understanding of the new life of divine grace. Baptism effects a real passage into Christ. All believers enjoy new life because they pass from the slavery of being *'in Adam'* into a new form of existence *'in the Lord.'* It is there that Paul meets them and rejoices with them in faith. He truly *'lives'* because of their presence to him. Given the experience of the Spirit in early christian communities (cf. 5:19), Paul's exuberance was not extravagant. Some exegetes suggest that Paul may be quoting a hymn sung by the Thessalonians, but no hard evidence exists to support that guess.

PROBLEMS TIMOTHY NOTED.
1 Thess 3:9-13.

> [9]For what thanksgiving can we render to God for you, for all the joy which we feel for your sake before our God, [10]praying earnestly night and day that we may see you face to face and supply what is lacking in your faith?
>
> [11]Now may our God and Father himself, and our Lord Jesus, direct our way to you; [12]and may the Lord make you increase and abound in love to one another and to all men, as we do to you, [13]so that he may establish your hearts unblamable in holiness before our God and Father, at the coming of our Lord Jesus with all his saints.

Without any formal break in structure Paul finally states the problems that trouble him about the church at Thessalonica on the basis of Timothy's report. He eases into them in such a subtle way that modern readers may fail to recognize what he is now doing. In his conversational and prayerful manner Paul is providing a brief introduction into the three topics that he wants to explain to his readers or—more accurately—to his hearers, because this letter would have originally been read to the community assembled together. Only one copy existed; so Paul had to unfold the topics as he approached them.

Paul was neither a professional writer nor theologian. He was a preacher and religious leader and organized his letters with pastoral awareness and creativity. Above all, he is an apostle deeply sensitive to his responsibility to face problems in communities he founded. He introduces the first topic with a question, *'For what thanksgiving can we render . . . ?'* It is a type of rhetorical question to arouse attention and to maintain the mood of concern that insures a receptive hearing for Paul's advice. Eugene LaVerdiere has captured well the tone and movement of this section in his brief introduction to the letter in *The BIBLE Today* 74 (November 1974).

Where does this question end? The RSV continues it through two verses as a single sentence. This is possible,

but a more natural punctuation, adopted in some translations, is to limit the question to verse 9 and to make verse 10
Paul's own answer. The question and answer technique is
used often in diatribes when the author dialogues with
readers. Read in this fashion, verse 9 becomes an exclama-
tion of apostolic *'joy'* and concern about their use of God's
gifts. They evoke a response of *'thanksgiving'* from Paul
because of his part in bringing them to the community. But
this apostrophe to God's goodness is more than a purely
rhetorical outburst. Paul unexpectedly cuts short his
rejoicing and turns back to his great longing to see them
(cf. 2:17). He repeats the same adverb *'eagerly'* (2:17) in an
extremely rare compound *'earnestly'* (3:10) to link these
passages. Unfortunately the change in wording in the
English translation obscures this link (cf. 5:13 for a companion form).

Paul does not answer his question with a declarative
sentence but with a participle. His response is to be *'praying
earnestly'* for them *'day and night'* (cf. 2:9). This lack of a
finite verb is no doubt why most editors include verse 10 in
the question. But finite verbs are not necessary in all sentences in the conversational style Paul uses here. This outburst is a real answer to his question because it tells the
Thessalonians both how much he was concerned about
them and that he would like to talk with them *'face to face'*
about shortcomings in the style of their faith. He expresses
this concern in a positive fashion; he wants to *'supply what
is lacking in your faith,'* a phrase found nowhere else in the
New Testament. It is Paul's way of giving an introductory
title to the part of this letter that will show them how to
correct their faulty understanding of the return of Jesus
in glory (4:13-5:11).

Before taking up that most difficult aspect of faith for
Greeks, Paul continues to express his desire to see them.
He does so in the form of a prayer that introduces their
other two needs that he is going to treat with them. In this
fashion he is able to justify his not coming to them per-
sonally at this time while communicating his deep concern

for their perseverance. Paul employs the optative three times in this prayer, although that mood was becoming rare in Greek. More important, his prayer addresses jointly the *'Father'* and the *'Lord Jesus'* as a single principle of activity by putting both the introductory adjective and the verb *'direct'* in the singular (cf. 2 Thess 2:16 for similar style).

When Paul writes the term *'God'* with the definite article as here, *ho theos* (the God), he focuses directly on the Father. In this passage he makes this identification explicit, *'our God and Father.'* The *'and'* is what is technically known as epexegetical, that is, it is purely explanatory to specify God as the Father. In Greek the *'our'* goes with *'Father,'* so that the phrase actually says "God and our Father" (also in v.13). One of the most profound revelations of the New Testament is that God is Father in a unique and transcendent way for all believers for they now live in a real sense in the Lord Jesus. The text is not to be equated with sexist language. As *'Father'* God exercises special care over believers and is attentive to their destiny. In using this title Paul is implicitly saying that he expects God to bring him to see the Thessalonians. But not now. And so he adds two more short prayers (fused into one in the RSV) in two specific areas that he is going to advise them about in the following sections of the letter.

Significantly, Paul addresses these two prayers to *'the Lord,'* that is, to Jesus in glory—implying that Jesus has divine power to sanctify their existence. While not confusing the roles of the Father and Jesus, from the beginning of his apostolic career Paul had an understanding of the unique transcendence of Jesus. The glorified Jesus possesses lordship over all creation. Paul petitions him for two needs for the Thessalonians:

(1) for the gift of *'love,'* without which they could not achieve the ideal set up for them. What Paul wants is that their love may grow until it is as strong as his love for them. This goal is obscured in the RSV's translation *'as we do to you,'* for Paul is not simply inviting them to be loving but to strive for the same intensity of love that he shows. Just

as in 1:6, he is setting himself up as model for their imitation of Christ. Paul can do this because he is fully confident of his calling and of God's working in him. Again he affirms that the love they receive in embracing faith in Christ is an abounding and increasing gift from the risen Lord Jesus, who wants them to direct it toward *'one another and to all men.'* This love that Jesus communicates is affectionate concern for the good of all as children of the Father. Paul has known this love, has shared it, and it is now impelling him to advance their growth in Christ. He will elaborate on the demands of this love in the section below on *'love of the brethren'* (4:9-12).

(2) The final petition of Paul is for a more specific effect of the Lord's presence in their lives, namely, that he keep their *'hearts unblamable in holiness'* in the Father's presence in anticipation of the Son's glorious *'coming.'* Paul speaks of the *'heart'* as center of intellectual and ethical action rather than as seat of emotions. In his anthropology persons think with their heart and thus reach their deepest convictions under the influence of God's grace (cf. 2:4). The image behind this prayer is that of the final judgment when all will be called to account for their lives. Paul prays that their personal holiness will then be manifest in their victory over Satan (cf. 3:5). As to the demands of this holiness, Paul will immediately spell them out in the following paragraph (4:1-8). In other words, Paul's three prayers will now be developed in reverse or chiasmic order as the instructions to the community (4:1-5:11).

The term *'holiness,'* common only in the Jewish bible before christian times, had a cultic origin. For Paul it embraced strong moral demands, as the following paragraph shows. He saw personal growth in holiness as a necessary prerequisite for being able to support others in love and so to prepare adequately for complete union with the *'Lord'* at his *'coming,'* that is, his parousia or glorious return, which they greatly desire (cf. 1:10). With the mention of this return Paul completes the triad of faith, love and hope for which he thanked God at the opening of this letter and from which all christian holiness takes shape.

The *'saints'* who come with Jesus may designate either the angels or deceased believers who will be present at the final judgment. Since Paul never uses the term *'saints'* for angels elsewhere, the presumption is that he is describing the heroes of sacred history as coming with the glorified Jesus.

In this section I have stressed the structure underlying the development of the paragraph because it is crucial for understanding the rest of the letter. Up to this point Paul has been recalling the past. Now he has taken the risk of challenging this young community at Thessalonica to embrace the demands of the cross at every level of existence. Paul recognized that they were at a crossroad. They had to push forward *'in the Lord'* or they would be overwhelmed by the enemy. He has been leading up to these instructions by means of his long opening thanksgiving, by his exhortations and by his personal sharing. Now he must complete his apostolic responsibility and make clear to the community how its members are to recommit themselves to the faith, love and hope they are called to celebrate.

Because all christians of every age face basically the same challenges and choices, early christians read, reread and shared this letter until it was incorporated into the official canon of scripture. Through this letter the apostle Paul continues to encourage and motivate believers about their destiny. This inspired writing continues to call the entire church to self-identity, especially when it is proclaimed in liturgical celebration. True faith offers sure hope.

PLEA FOR MORAL RESPONSIBILITY.
1 Thess 4:1-8.

> **4** Finally, brethren, we beseech and exhort you in the Lord Jesus, that as you learned from us how you ought to live and to please God, just as you are doing, you do so

more and more. ²For you know what instructions we gave you through the Lord Jesus. ³For this is the will of God, your sanctification: that you abstain from unchastity; ⁴that each one of you know how to take a wife for himself˟ in holiness and honor, ⁵not in the passion of lust like heathen who do not know God; ⁶that no man transgress, and wrong his brother in this matter,ª because the Lord is an avenger in all these things, as we solemnly forewarned you. ⁷For God has not called us for uncleanness, but in holiness. ⁸Therefore whoever disregards this, disregards not man but God, who gives his Holy Spirit to you.

˟Or *how to control his own body*
ªOr *defraud his brother in business*

Paul now develops the implications of the last of his three prayers. He spells out what it means for them to have *'hearts unblamable in holiness,'* for this is the status he wants them to possess when Jesus Christ comes as universal judge. He still retains his caution by using three elements of phatic communion—that is personal touches added solely to keep channels of communication open so that they will receive his advice. The RSV version does not handle this aspect well. It begins by translating his opening particle as *'finally.'* It is true that the term can be used to introduce the final section of a literary development. But it is also used to mark a transfer of direction or to introduce a new direction of thought. And that is its function here. Paul alerts readers to be attentive and open to what he is going to say. In English perhaps the best translation is "so," especially when the next term in Greek (*oun*, then) is omitted, as in the RSV. Both of these terms are phatic elements, and they are followed by a third, the vocative *'brethren,'* an address that communicates Paul's concern.

The double verb *'we beseech and exhort you'* maintains the same mood of urgency. This is the only time the combination occurs in the New Testament, although it is found in

Greek papyri texts. And to ground this entreaty in faith Paul reminds them that he pleads with them *'in the Lord Jesus.'* Both he and they are *'in the Lord'* as the sphere of their spiritual journey, as the meeting place of mutual support, and as the source of power needed to carry out the advice he is about to give.

The first two verses of this paragraph remind the Thessalonians that they have *'learned from'* Paul that they have the necessary divine power to accomplish what he is about to tell them to do. Actually the verb in Greek says they have "received what has been handed down." It is the verb from which the technical term "tradition" is formed. Paul affirms that he is simply restating the true faith in the following directives. Although cast in the form of a polite request, these verses imply the imperative: "do better." In his phrase, *'do so more and more,'* Paul employs the same verb translated above as *'abound'* (3:12). The RSV version also eliminates the image of walking to describe christian lifestyle (cf. on 2:12). Paul assures them they do not have to fear; he adds nothing to the *'instructions'* he gave them earlier. He looks upon the good news in the same way the Jews considered the law of Moses—as the life-giving will of God. By submitting to these instructions believers receive divine power to put them into effect.

What this life-giving *'will of God'* is for them Paul now states explicitly and emphatically. It is their *'sanctification,'* a term he uses three times here; it is from the same root as the word translated *'holiness'* in 3:13. *'Sanctification,'* a term confined to the Judeo-christian tradition, is the total process —including moral development—by which God purifies and transforms believers into his true worshipers. The cultic image of consecration, setting a person or place apart for cult, underlies this term, but *'sanctification'* takes on a wide range of conduct when applied to christians. It is God's way of making them fitting participants in the life he gives by his *'Holy Spirit.'*

The specific area in which Paul sees the need for improvement is their sexual ethics. First of all, he recalls that the '*will of God*' demands they '*abstain from unchastity,*' that is, from all forms of illicit sexual conduct. Then Paul adds another more specific directive, the meaning of which is still disputed. The RSV understands it as referring to unchastity in marriage, '*that each one of you know how to take a wife for himself,*' but offers an alternate possibility in the note, '*how to control his own body.*' (The reading of the note is put into the text of the edition edited by the Catholic Biblical Association of Great Britain.) The former translation seems to satisfy the context, especially since Paul makes mention of the responsibilities of christian husbands toward their wives, namely, to treat them with a sense of being accountable to the Lord for transgressions '*in this matter.*' Wives are worthy of '*honor.*'

But this solution is not certain because, to get this meaning, the RSV assumes that the Greek word of the text that literally means "vessel" (v.4) is to be understood as '*wife*'— an assumption that is not proved. Since the time of the fathers of the church, commentators have disputed whether this word should be understood as wife or body. In fact, a third possibility exists and is adopted in the New American Bible, which takes vessel as a euphemism for the male organ and interprets Paul as speaking about sexual self-control.

In whatever translation is adopted Paul calls for a more demanding code of christian sexual conduct. This demand had become a problem for believers in Thessalonica. After the first fervor of conversion with an overpowering experience of the gift of the Holy Spirit, many believers were now going through a period of trial and finding it difficult to meet the demands of their new way of life. Paul warns them against returning to their former status as pagans when they were subject to '*the passion of lust.*' He equates lack of control over sexual passions with the situation of being '*heathen who do not know God.*' By '*knowing God*' Paul means relating to him in the religious and experiential sense of enjoying a living and loving relationship with the author of the moral order. He saw paganism's refusal to accept the '*will of God*' the creator as the origin of a torrent of sins that engulfed humanity (cf. Rom 1:24-32).

Lack of chastity in marriage is a serious offense against mutual brotherly love; it is a form of deceit that destroys marriages. In addition, it makes men *'transgress'* (a term found only here in the New Testament) the law of God. No wonder that *'the Lord is an avenger of all these things.'* When? In the final judgment, a reality never far from Paul's mind. He hastens to soften the force of this demand by stating that he is not telling them something new. He had *'forewarned'* them when he preached the good news there.

Two aspects of this warning may appear strange to modern readers: (1) that it is directed only to males. No doubt Paul envisioned them as taking the initiative in sexual misconduct by seducing females, whose lives were more confined and restricted; (2) that Paul works out of what is today considered a low level of motivation, namely, the threat of punishment by the Lord as *'an avenger.'* But Paul goes on to balance this negative approach by offering more lofty motivation at the end of the paragraph. Their life of faith is a special gift. God lovingly *'called'* them, inviting them to *'holiness,'* a higher form of conduct. This call is important and not to be ignored because our destiny is subject to his power. God's call is not empty for he *'gives his Holy Spirit'* to believers. Paul may be alluding to a saying of Jesus that to despise him is to despise the one who sent him (cf. Lk 10:6). To return to a life of sexual excess is a form of despising the Spirit as living principle of this new life.

After alternating between the Lord Jesus and the Father, for the first time in his letters Paul mentions the Holy Spirit explicitly. Although extremely rare in the Hebrew bible, the Holy Spirit is a key revelation of the New Testament. Ordinarily his presence becomes known only through the actions of believers. Here the action of the Holy Spirit in believers is manifest by the holiness that the Father achieves in them through him. God's desires are not empty but effective. In this case they result in the gift of the Holy Spirit who makes their holiness possible. This paragraph, therefore, is trinitarian in that is calls attention to the activity of Father, Son and Holy Spirit in their growth *'in holiness.'*

Paul's ardent appeal implies that the Thessalonians had a vivid experience of the Holy Spirit in connection with his original preaching (cf. 5:19). He can appeal to that presence with the assurance that it will exert a strong influence on their conduct. Obviously Paul would not have put these warnings in the letter if Timothy had not called attention to problems in the area of sex. Yet, up to this point Paul has been lavish in his praise of the Thessalonians. He took a gentle stance toward them, in keeping with the image that he is their *'nurse'* (2:7). But now he presses them on to a full commitment to the *'will of God'* in ethical conduct.

Some commentators interpret verse 6 in a more general sense that Paul is instructing the Thessalonians to treat others justly in business dealings and to avoid avarice and fraud. (Thus the variant reading: "defraud his brother in business," RSV note.) But the movement of the paragraph and especially the warnings against *'uncleanness'* in verse 7 favor retaining the specific sense of sexual integrity throughout.

EXHORTATION TO MUTUAL LOVE.
1 Thess 4:9-12.

> [9]But concerning love of the brethren you have no need to have any one write to you, for you yourselves have been taught by God to love one another; [10]and indeed you do love all the brethren throughout Macedonia. But we exhort you, brethren, to do so more and more, [11]to aspire to live quietly, to mind your own affairs, and to work with your hands, as we charged you; [12]so that you may command the respect of outsiders, and be dependent on nobody.

Paul now moves to his second area of concern where their conduct needs improvement, namely, mutual love. In this short paragraph he develops his earlier prayer that they *'increase and abound in love'* (3:13). Here he prefers to speak in general terms rather than to go into concrete details.

Possibly he delegated Timothy to deal with specific cases when he was with the Thessalonians. This brief answer has several unusual words not typical of Paul. Perhaps he did not find this approach effective. Or perhaps the situation in this community with its vivid expectations of Christ's return in glory called for special instructions.

Paul introduces the topic by using a figure of speech. He asserts that he really does not have to write about the subject. This is a technique to discuss a topic that a writer for some reason hesitates to mention. In his prayer he spoke to them of *'love to one another'* (3:12), but now he changes to *'love of the brethren.'* In Greek this phrase is a single word *philadelphia*. This word appears first in the fourth century B.C. but never appears in translations of the Hebrew bible. In employing it New Testament writers change its meaning from love for blood relatives to affection for members of the believing community, who are ordinarily referred to as brothers (cf. v. 10).

Paul says he does not have to deal with *'love of the brethren'* because they have been *'taught by God'* in this area. Again the English phrase is a single compound Greek word found for the first time in literature here. Possibly Paul coined it. What did he have in mind? Two lines of approach are plausible: either (1) he wanted to recall what Jeremiah saw as a characteristic of the New Covenant (Jer 31:34). No person would teach another but rather God would be teacher of all within their hearts. If Paul had this text in mind, he affirms that the christian life is the fruit of grace, the gift of God from which flows love for one another; or (2) Paul presents his task as apostle as bringing his converts to an awareness of God's special care for them in sending his Son Jesus (cf. 4:2). In believing and obeying Jesus they already experience him as their Savior. His life and voluntary death are ultimately the great teachers of love. Implied in the example of Jesus is that unique command to love as he loved, even unto death (cf. Jn 13:34).

Once more Paul continues not by appealing to logic but by an act of phatic communion. He keeps the channels of communication open with the same idiom *kai gar* used in 3:4, but translated here with more feeling as *'and indeed.'* He does not lord it over them but reminds them that they already possess divine grace because they are practicing true christian concern toward *'all the brethren throughout Macedonia.'* It is not clear how they were in touch with communities at such a distance if Paul wrote only a few months after visiting them. Hence, this statement has been used by some commentators to date this letter from Paul's third missionary journey.

He quickly brings this short paragraph to a close with another fervent exhortation, repeating two verbs already found in verse 1: *'exhort'* and *'do so more and more.'* Paul spells out what this *'love of the brothers'* means for them in their particular situation. This turns out to be a collection of wide-ranging forms of conduct: tranquility, greater self-reliance, doing their own thing (RSV's *'mind your own affairs'* does not convey the positive thrust of this command) and earning their own living by manual labor. Paul conceives all forms of good example as expressions of brotherly love. In urging them to *'be dependent on nobody'* Paul is not advocating Stoic self-control but rather unselfish christian service. In fact, instead of *'nobody,'* the Greek text can also mean *'dependent on nothing,'* an attitude that Paul recommended as establishing deeper trust in God alone (cf. Phil 4:13).

This set of advice reflects Paul's concern that christians do not disturb social tranquility. The harmonious community on all levels of existence would be a powerful witness to the pagan world. The lifestyle he recommends was especially needed in a community with vivid eschatological expectations. Paul promises that if they obey the advice he offers they will enjoy internal harmony as *'brethren'* and will bear fruitful witness of God's wisdom before their pagan neighbors. The special power of God's love as manifest in *'love of the brethren'* is to create the new age that Jeremiah had predicted. Through this love God reigns in the heart of each believer and offers hope of the final victory of good over evil.

Some of these qualities are repeated in 2 Thess 3:6-12, which seems to be an expansion of this paragraph in the light of subsequent developments within the community. These words of advice of Paul provide insight into his understanding of the paradoxical working of divine grace in all areas of human existence. Grace creates a spirit of complete trust in God's power and willingness to do *'more and more'* for others.

THE CERTAINTY OF CHRIST'S COMING.
1 Thess 4:13-18.

> [13]But we would not have you ignorant, brethren, concerning those who are asleep, that you may not grieve as others do who have no hope. [14]For since we believe that Jesus died and rose again, even so, through Jesus, God will bring with him those who have fallen asleep. [15]For this we declare to you by the word of the Lord, that we who are alive, who are left until the coming of the Lord, shall not precede those who have fallen asleep. [16]For the Lord himself will descend from heaven with a cry of command, with the archangel's call, and with the sound of the trumpet of God. And the dead in Christ will rise first; [17]then we who are alive, who are left, shall be caught up together with them in the clouds to meet the Lord in the air; and so we shall always be with the Lord. [18]Therefore comfort one another with these words.

The lack of any apparent connection between this paragraph and the one immediately preceding is explicable if we recognize that Paul has reached the point of addressing the first problem he spoke about in the prayer that introduces this part of the letter (cf. 3:9-10). He now clarifies how their faith falls short. It is because they misunderstood two key elements of the christian message. So he is going to explain these truths in two paragraphs, both of which fall under the words *'concerning those who are asleep,'* which act as a kind of title. Unfortunately the division into chapters made in the middle ages obscures the unity of this development for readers of modern editions of the New Testament. Paul's purpose here is not to develop abstract dogmatic theses but to perform his pastoral duty of making up what is lacking in their faith (cf. 3:10). The two insights he conveys are: (1) that physical death—to *'have fallen asleep'*—is no bar to sharing in the victory of the risen Lord Jesus (4:13-18); (2) how they are to *'comfort'* or encourage one another to prepare in hope for the return of the Lord Jesus (5:1-11).

Implied in the first instruction is that Jesus is now in the condition of being *'Lord,'* that is, his glorious existence is life-giving for his followers. Once more Paul opens with a literary figure. He uses litotes or understatement. *'But we would not have you ignorant, brethren'* means that he is anxious to clear up a point that is important for their faith. This manner of approaching the subject together with his repetition of the title *'brethren'* continues his care to evoke a positive response from them by using phatic communion.

Paul makes every effort to eliminate the fears he senses in this young church; their enflamed apocalyptic expectations are now chilled by the death of some members. His topic is the fate of *'those who are asleep,'* that is, christians who have already died or who will die before Jesus comes. Sleep is a common euphemism for death in both Jewish and Greek literature. The issue raised by this topic is the power of their new faith and the certainty of the hope it promises. In becoming christians they committed their lives to the transcendent destiny they received as gift from God *'in Christ.'* Their faith encompasses a hope that takes away the sting of death through which unbelievers face bitter grief.

Paul assures the Thessalonians that they have no reason to fear. Believers remain 'in Christ' whether they are still in this life or undergo physical death. Death cannot take away their hope because the risen life is simply a fuller experience of the grace they receive through faith and baptism. Paul explains this aspect of faith and its implications for their lives only briefly. Readers cannot help but think that these brief instructions were meant to be augmented by Timothy's oral explanations. He will help them recognize that they are different from the pagans *'who have no hope.'* Paul's self-imposed limitations in this explanation present difficulties for modern readers because it is cast in apocalyptic style. Therefore, there is no carefully reasoned eschatology (teaching on the final destiny and situation of humanity) in these verses.

As often happens with Paul, his thinking rushes faster than his words and he omits elements of the development of his ideas in verse 14. Since he does not complete his explanation of the status of the dead *'in Christ,'* he creates an elipsis. Readers must fill in his comparison with a phrase like "then we will not lose hope." The RSV misplaces the phrase *'through Jesus',* which in Greek is linked to *'die.'* It is only those who "die through Jesus" that *'God will bring with him'* to glory. To "die through Jesus" is not only to die for his sake but in a way that shares in the power of his lordship to give life. By this power *'God will bring'* believers into his glory along with the risen Christ. Paul does not say when this will take place. What he stresses is that even in death believers remain *'in Christ'* and are destined for glory.

Here Paul does not try to explain how this is accomplished, but rather gives the basis for hope that it will be done. Our belief that *'Jesus died and rose again,'* an integral part of the christian creed, is the basis of hope. How are these linked? The manner by which Christ returned to his Father's glory—by way of the cross and resurrection —reveals to believers God's power to triumph over evil both in the case of Jesus and in the lives of all who believe in him. Hence, not only is the cross their *'lot'* (3:3) but also Christ's risen glory. True faith includes firm hope of enjoying this glory and a lifestyle of freedom from sin that is both a witness to and a sharing in that glory. Since physical death cannot separate believers from God, there is no reason to be disturbed by the death of believers.

Paul does not speak about the condition of *'those who are asleep'* until Christ comes in glory. He simply states that their hope about the equality of status for both the living and the dead at *'the coming of the Lord'* rests upon *'the word of the Lord.'* This assertion causes a problem on two counts:

(1) that such a statement is not attributed to Jesus in any of the gospels. Of course, christian literature refers to sayings of Jesus not recorded in the canonical gospels, and so this absence is not an insoluble difficulty. Furthermore, Paul may have been using the phrase *'the word of the Lord'* for a saying of an early christian prophet. Since these prophets acted under the influence of the Holy Spirit, their sayings would be attributed to the Lord Jesus as giver of the Spirit.

(2) that Paul's statement implies he will be alive at the *'coming'* of the Lord (cf. also v.17). Certainly Paul at this time wanted to be alive to meet Jesus and his early preaching communicated an enthusiasm for this return, as is clear from the problems he encountered with the Thessalonians. As time went on, however, Paul came to see more clearly the nature of that *'coming'* as not another event within history but as a history-shattering reality that communicates the fulness of life. So in later writings he treats the ultimate victory of Christ in terms less likely to be misunderstood.

Paul enhances his encouragement by using a vivid apocalyptic description. The style would appeal to the enthusiastic Thessalonians but can easily be misunderstood by modern readers who are not at home in apocalyptic imagery and want to convert it into historical details. In symbolic language Paul lists three features of Christ's coming, without specifying how they relate to each other: (1) *'a cry of command.'* This phrase translates the single word for *'command'* of the Greek text, a word never found elsewhere in the bible. Paul does not say who utters it. (2) *'the archangel's call.'* Archangels are never mentioned either in the Hebrew bible or in the other books incorporated in the christian bible as part of its Old Testament, although loud sounds and heavenly voices appear often in biblical tradition (cf. Rev 19:1). (3) *'the trumpet of God.'* Paul again mentions a trumpet blast when he talks about the glorious return of the Lord in 1 Cor 15:52. A horn is linked to divine judgment in Is 27:13 and Zech 9:14. Whether these are meant to be three distinct details or simply symbols of a transcendent event is not clear. In fact, even the Thessalonians seem to have had difficulty understanding Paul's treatment of the parousia because 2 Thess testifies that they needed further instruction in this matter.

These elements are meant to be interpreted in apocalyptic fashion. They are not historical details of passing events but are Paul's way of saying that resurrection and passing beyond death to be with Christ create a new form of existence. This new life is a gift that comes from outside human powers through a special divine intervention. Risen life is *'in Christ'* as the Lord who is no longer subject to created limitations. In him God creates the humanity of the new age. Rather than being a cause for fear among believers death provides God with the occasion to display his vivifying power on behalf of both the ones *'who are left until the coming of the Lord'* as well as *'those who have fallen asleep.'* These dead will rise *'first.'* This term *'first'* is used in the sense of a more startling display of divine power rather than as the start of a series of events at the last judgment because Paul affirms in 1 Cor 15:52 that the entire transformation will happen *'in the twinkling of an eye.'*

Modern scientific mentality finds it almost impossible to deal with apocalyptic imagery without trying to translate it into logical concepts. But the heart of Paul's message is to assure his readers that *'we shall always be with the Lord.'* To have passed through the experience of death does not alter this hope in any way. *'To be with the Lord'* is the result of a transformation that boggles the human imagination and so must ultimately be believed solely *'on the word of the Lord.'* Paul uses images from descriptions of past saving interventions of God for his chosen people as described in the bible. Because early christians saw the resurrection of Jesus and his return in glory as the climax of all God's saving interventions, they applied the traditional biblical imagery to them.

In the final section of this paragraph Paul makes use of popular biblical cosmology to describe this coming. Heaven is a physical abode above the dome of the sky. The *'clouds'* are instruments God uses to manifest his presence (cf. Dan 7:13; Mt 26:64; Rev 1:7; 14:14-16). Here, however, Paul sees the believers as also enveloped *'in the clouds'* because they receive a share in the status of the glorified Jesus. They participate in the divine power that Jesus as Lord is able to communicate to others. This meeting is a solemn, saving encounter. Paul indicates that it takes place *'in the air'* without describing it further. He quickly drops attempts to describe it as an event (known in later theology as the rapture) and moves into the real goal of this paragraph—mutual encouragement. The Thessalonians must pass beyond the state of those who *'have no hope'* and *'comfort one another with these words,'* namely, that believers will always *'be with the Lord.'*

The faith by which they are *'in Christ'* in this life leads to the hope of being *'with the Lord'* always. This mutual hope enables members of this young community to *'comfort'* one another, to resist pagan threats and values and to put off selfish ways of living in this world. The command to *'comfort one another'* brings Paul to explain, in the next paragraph, how they can do so. There he will address certain misapprehensions about the return of Jesus. Paul will use that instruction as his springboard for a rousing exhortation that closes much like this one (compare 4:18 and 5:11, noting that the words translated as *'comfort'* and *'encourage'* are the same verb in Greek).

DRAWING COURAGE FROM CHRIST'S RETURN. 1 Thess 5:1-11.

5 But as to the times and the seasons, brethren, you have no need to have anything written to you. [2]For you yourselves know well that the day of the Lord will come like a thief in the night. [3]When people say, "There is peace and security," then sudden destruction will come upon them as travail comes upon a woman with child, and there will be no escape. [4]But you are not in darkness, brethren, for that day to surprise you like a thief. [5]For you are all sons of light and sons of the day; we are not of the night or of darkness. [6]So then let us not sleep, as others do, but let us keep awake and be sober. [7]For those who sleep sleep at night, and those who get drunk are drunk at night. [8]But, since we belong to the day, let us be sober, and put on the breastplate of faith and love, and for a helmet the hope of salvation. [9]For God has not destined us for wrath, but to obtain salvation through our Lord Jesus Christ, [10]who died for us so that whether we wake or sleep we might live with him. [11]Therefore encourage one another and build one another up, just as you are doing.

Having reassured them that Christ's return will confirm the hope of all believers, Paul takes up certain misunderstandings about it that prevailed at Thessalonica. But he soon turns to an instruction on how to translate their hope into a program of christian living to prepare for that coming. This paragraph illustrates how Paul's ethical stance grew organically out of his vision of faith in Jesus Christ. He wanted all of his disciples to achieve this same spiritual integration because it offers deep joy, peace and stability in trial. These are gifts of God but they also make demands on believers, as he will show.

Evidently the community had been involved in speculation and discussion about how to predict the glorious return of Jesus which they felt was historically imminent. They proposed all kinds of methods which Paul does not want to criticize directly. So again he begins with the literary figure of introducing his topic by saying that they have *'no need to have anything written'* about *'the times and the seasons'* (cf. 4:9). This style provides an opportunity to make comments in a friendly way and to turn attention to fruitful spiritual concerns. Repetition of the address 'brethren' fosters a spirit of trust and maintains Paul's conversational style. He directs their thoughts from useless speculation to the reality of the *'salvation'* offered through the death and resurrection of Jesus.

The two words *'times'* and *'seasons'* appear together often. In itself *'times'* refers to the way ordinary duration is measured—what C. H. Giblin calls 'clock and calendar' time. *'Seasons'* are fixed moments in time for decision or celebration. The term often has eschatological significance, as here (cf. Acts 1:7). In Jewish tradition the last days were viewed as moments for the fulfilment of God's plan, the climax of preordained periods of time. Jesus modified this tradition by proclaiming that the Lord's coming would be *'like a thief in the night'* (cf. Mt 24:42-44; 2 Pt 3:10; Rev 3:3). Paul applies the image to *'the day of the Lord'* (simply *'day'* in v. 4) in a curious blending of images that is not without irony—whether deliberate or not.

'The day of the Lord' is an expression that goes back to early prophets (cf. Amos 5:18). The image went through a long evolution before becoming popular in apocalyptic writings like the Book of Enoch, which influenced the New Testament. The apocalyptic use of the term served to keep alive hope in the final victory of God's plan and to encourage trust among the Jews in times of crisis. In

usurping this term for the glorious return of Jesus Paul identifies his coming as an eschatological event, one that breaks in from beyond calendar time and so one that cannot be measured by this world's standards. Such a way of looking at the return of Jesus provides context for Paul's earlier assertion about those who would be alive at this coming (4:15). Humans cannot pin down this event or predict it. Paul simply accepts it as certain and moves rapidly to draw practical ethical conclusions from its mysterious power.

Before his hearers have a chance to notice it, Paul has shifted his focus from their questions to a warning not to let down their guard against the 'tempter' (3:5), who is master of *'darkness.'* No matter how calm the situation seems, believers are always exposed to temptation. Thus, to rely on their own resources is to expose themselves to *'sudden destruction.'* Their only hope to avoid falling prey to the *'thief'* is not to be a person of *'darkness.'* To describe the power of darkness Paul employs the graphic image found in the prophets of the *'travail'* that *'comes upon a woman with child'* (cf. also Jn 16:21). He applies this image to the cosmic upheavals that worried the Thessalonians.

The proverb he quotes, *'There is peace and security,'* apparently alludes to the unbelieving attitude of the citizens of Jerusalem at the time of Jeremiah (cf. Jer 6:14), unless he is simply speaking about the practice of false prophets who seek to gain favor by optimistic promises. The citizens of Jerusalem at the time of Jeremiah refused to believe that the Lord would allow his chosen city to be destroyed and so ignored his pleas for repentance. Paul warns these young christians against failing to respond to the Lord's warnings. They must be truly *'day'* people, *'awake and sober.'*

Paul sees a gigantic conflict going on between the cosmic forces of good and evil, God and Satan, symbolized by *'light'* and *'darkness.'* But instead of becoming too involved in this imagery as apocalyptic writers tended to do, Paul shifts to moral exhortation. He sidesteps what he

considers to be irrelevant speculation and puts before
their minds the traumatic reality of inescapable judgment.
Again he buttresses his appeal with the address of *'brethren'*
and an assurance that they do not have to fear because they
are *'not in darkness.'* On the contrary, he reminds them
that they are *'all sons of the light and sons' of the day,'*
shifting the meaning of *'day'* from the expression *'day of
the Lord'* to the metaphorical sense of uprightness, not
found elsewhere in the bible.

By contrast, the phrase *'sons of (the) light'* is found in
Lk 16:8 and Jn 12:36, and *'children of light'* in Eph 5:8.
Members of the Qumran community were called "sons of
light" and were taught to hate and wage war against the
"sons of darkness." These expressions are examples of the
way Semitic languages combine "sons" or "children"
with the metaphorical use of light to proclaim that such
persons live by the spiritual power of truth showing them
how to discern and seek good (cf. Rom 13:11-14). Paul
puts stress on these images by stating them in both positive and negative forms. In the second case he passes from
second to first person, identifying himself with the Thessalonians in another expression of confidence. The last
part of this paragraph draws ethical conclusions (vv. 6-8)
and then provides further motivation (vv. 9-10). This
brings Paul to a final word of exhortation, similar to that
in the companion section (cf. 4:18) but stronger because
of an additional instruction.

The *'so then'* opening these ethical conclusions is a
common idiom indicating inference. The image of *'sleep'*
for spiritual laziness is found in pagan Greek literature
and in the hymn cited in Eph 5:14. (In v.10 *'sleep'* is the
image for death as in 4:14, but in v.7 *'sleep'* is used in its
ordinary physical sense.) The *'others'* who *'sleep'* by their
sloth are equivalent to those *'who have no hope'* in 4:13.
As I noted above, Paul sees true ethical integrity as
growing organically from the life of faith he planted
among them. So his exhortation to *'keep awake and be
sober'* looks at their eschatological goal (cf. 1 Pt 5:8).

'*Sober,*' implying freedom from all forms of excess, conforms to the Hellenistic love of moderation. Paul goes on to single out two areas explicitly for moderation: sleep and drink. In view of his warnings against '*unchastity*' (4:3-6), the term '*sleep*' may imply that his first warning is for moderation in the area of sex (cf. Ps 127:2-3). Excess in either of these areas is a sign of belonging to the sphere of '*night*' and of having failed in apocalyptic watchfulness. In verse 8 Paul not only changes the image but returns to the first person to join with them in spirit in their struggle. He sees victory as grounded in the triad of faith, love and hope that he praised in them in his opening thanksgiving (cf. 1:3). These are described as part of the armor a christian is to wear in the battle for '*salvation.*'

Paul does not use this imagery well. The '*breastplate*' is both '*faith*' and '*love.*' Where '*breastplate*' is used elsewhere in the bible (Is 59:14-17; Wis 5:18; Eph 6:14-17), it symbolizes justice. B. Rigaux provides a table in his commentary to show how the imagery shifted in these texts. Paul insisted earlier in this letter on the ethical dimension of faith (cf. 4:1-12). He maintains that thrust by linking '*faith*' and '*love*'; from these flow the new creation. '*Hope of salvation*' is symbolized by a '*helmet.*' In Eph 6:17 the '*helmet*' is '*salvation.*' In using the figures of light and darkness, Paul uses images rooted in biblical tradition. But why does he shift images so much? Perhaps because this imagery belongs to prophetic teaching on '*the day of the Lord,*' and Paul may have intended to recall that tradition. The combat imagery also recalls biblical teaching on the holy war, popular in the Qumran community; it is appropriate for fighting spiritual sloth.

God's mercy in calling the Thessalonians to believe in the gospel was his way of separating them from those who will experience his '*wrath,*' mentioned in 2:16 and called '*the wrath to come*' in 1:10. Their '*hope of salvation*' is not to be empty idleness but an active participation to '*obtain salvation*' (cf. 2 Thess 2:14). The nature of the two weapons shows that this holy war is not an offensive battle on the part of believers. On the contrary, they protect what God sends upon them as gifts *'through our Lord Jesus Christ.'* The momentum of the mention of his name carries Paul along to add that Jesus died *'for us.'* This is the earliest witness to the redemptive nature of the death of Jesus. Significantly it comes in a matter-of-fact way without comment. This profound truth was already part of christian tradition. Paul moves on to encourage his hearers to respond to the gift of *'salvation'* they receive through Jesus' great act of obedience to his Father in order that they may come to *'live with him'* forever.

Paul wants to repeat his teaching that all believers—whether still in this earthly life *'in Christ'* or already in the sleep of death—are never separated from their risen Lord. So he brings this argument to a close by another exhortation to courage. He adds two new items: (1) *'to build one another up.'* This is his first use of the building metaphor that appears frequently in the Corinthian correspondence. He represents the responsibility of edification as a mutual task to be undertaken by all. (2) that they are already doing well. After such a long exhortation this final phrase is surprising, *'just as you are doing.'* Paul means it as an expression of trust. And perhaps deep down this is why Paul does not give detailed answers to their problems as reported by Timothy. Instead, he repeats the saving significance of the passion of Jesus for them. They are open to the Spirit and willing to cooperate in patient hope.

ADVICE FOR LIVING AS CHRISTIANS.
1 Thess 5:12-22.

> [12]But we beseech you, brethren, to respect those who labor among you and are over you in the Lord and admonish you, [13]and to esteem them very highly in love because of their work. Be at peace among yourselves. [14]And we exhort you, brethren, admonish the idlers, encourage the fainthearted, help the weak, be patient

with them all. [15]See that none of you repays evil for evil,
but always seek to do good to one another and to all.
[16]Rejoice always, [17]pray constantly, [18]give thanks in all
circumstances; for this is the will of God in Christ Jesus
for you. [19]Do not quench the Spirit, [20]do not despise
prophesying, [21]but test everything; hold fast what is good,
[22]abstain from every form of evil.

Having dealt with the three serious questions facing the
young church at Thessalonica, Paul now closes his letter
quickly with a staccato-like series of admonitions that
provide his evaluation of the living situation of an early
christian community as it made its first organizational
efforts. Rigaux sees them as Paul's application of the
theme of *'building up'* (v.11). Yet it is difficult to follow
him in seeing four themes: community, order, fervor and
charity. More correctly he describes this paragraph as an
"explosion" of Paul's love for this church. Although these
pieces of advice seem to be unconnected, they are linked
together by Paul's overarching eschatological thrust and
concern. Careful reflection on them can lead to a better
understanding of the dynamic of christian ethics in every
age.

Once more Paul addresses the whole community as
'brethren.' Now for the first time he indicates that it has
some sort of leadership cadre, which he describes by three
types of activities. The first is general; this group consists
of *'those who labor among you.'* The other two are more
specific, indicating that the leaders *'are over you in the Lord'*
and *'admonish'* the members. Did Paul look upon these
leaders as a distinct group? It is not possible to decide.
The vagueness of their tasks shows that a special ministry
was just beginning in this church. But it is beginning, and
that is an important step for an eschatological community.
Since Paul does not have titles for these authority figures,
it is probable that they were not yet fixed. So we cannot
affirm what kind of organization existed. New Testament

writings indicate that a variety of local community struc-
tures existed simultaneously. Important for understanding
the nature of the church as a whole is this movement toward
specialization despite belief in the imminent return of
Jesus. Believers lived on many levels of reality. The eschatological thrust did not take away their concern for daily
living. Christian life is both eschatological and personal
in thrust, and all its activities center on *'the will of God in
Christ Jesus,'* (v.18) in hope that *'we might live with him'*
(v.10). This is an attitude that Paul wishes for them so
strongly that he begins his final exhortation with the emphatic *'we beseech you,'* the same verb used to introduce
his first piece of advice on how to pursue holiness (4:1).

This continuing tone of deference may sound out of place
in modern democratic society, but it expresses Paul's deep
belief that God's grace is the source of freedom and moral
responsibility. As an apostle his primary task was to remind
them by his own words and actions of the Spirit's activity
in their lives. He did not dictate to the Spirit but kept himself
open to this divine presence in every believer. He wanted to
foster the same openness in them so that they would use
God's gifts to *'build one another up'* in love. So Paul now
urges all to *'respect'* the members who have undertaken to
'labor among' them in a special role. The word in Greek
translated *'respect'* is the common verb *'know'* that takes
on the special meaning of understanding and appreciating
one another (cf. 1:4).

The verb translated *'are over'* can also mean "are concerned about" (cf. Rom 12:8). This meaning blends better
with the other two activities of the leaders. It points to an
unstructured situation in contrast to the clear picture of
'elders' sharing authority in 1 Tim 5:17. True, these leaders
'admonish,' but later in this paragraph Paul tells all to
'admonish' the idlers (v.14). Toward the leaders Paul gives
only one directive, namely, *'to esteem them very highly in
love because of their work.'* The phrase *'very highly'* is too
weak for the adverb translated in 3:10 as *'earnestly.'* It is

rare and means "at the highest level." Since community members know what their leaders do, Paul does not describe their work and we are left to speculate. And commentators do just that—but without much foundation in the text. Such speculation is a topic reserved for specialized articles rather than for this type of commentary.

Paul goes on with an admonition of mutual *'peace.'* He employs the present imperative, which means, "Keep the peace among yourselves." They should foster all those qualities implied in the Hebrew word *shalom*, the fulness of God's blessings. Paul immediately becomes more specific and refers to situations resulting from the lack of faith he set out to correct above (cf. 3:10). He meets these problems with four commands, placed together without conjunctions in the stylistic figure of asyndeton. The style is oratorical rather than a logical analysis of needs.

He imposes on the community as a whole four tasks: (1) *'admonish the idlers.'* The term actually means "the disorderly," but the context indicates that their fault is a failure to get prepared for the return of Jesus (cf. 4:11). That event remained a problem for the Thessalonians and is dealt with more fully in 2 Thess 3:6-11.

(2) *'encourage the fainthearted.'* This is exactly what Paul said he did when he worked among them (cf. 2:13).

(3) *'help the weak.'* The verb in Greek conveys the idea of showing interest in and so taking care of the persons concerned. He is speaking of the *'weak'* in faith, not the physically infirm. Paul never repeats this admonition in later letters.

(4) *'be patient with them all.'* The Greek text does not have the *'them,'* but urges, *'Be patient with all.'* Paul saw patience as one of the first qualities of love (1 Cor 13:4). He calls it *'fruit of the Spirit'* (Gal 5:22). Patience is the form of endurance that bears with evils in the hope of enjoying God's victory. In biblical tradition it is a mark of God's dealing with his creatures. The kind of patience Paul demands is a gift of God through Jesus. Believers

have opportunities to practice it in every situation. They do so by carrying out the next command of Paul not to repay *'evil for evil.'* Patience is prominent in the moral admonition of Paul in Rom 12:17 in practically the same terms as here. Possibly this was a traditional christian catechesis based on the scriptural texts found in Romans.

Paul now moves on to the positive demands of christian love. Believers must always *'seek to do good'*: first within the community and then *'to all.'* The RSV does not convey the urgency with which Paul expresses this piece of advice. The Greek text reads more like, "Run after what is good; make that your priority." They should be anxious to witness God's presence to them. How? By observing the next three commands that follow without any connective:

(1) *'rejoice always,'* a command that Paul never repeats in exactly the same terms—the phrase in Phil 4:4 means "goodby"—although he often urges christians to rejoice, because he sees joy as a fruit of the Spirit's presence (cf. Gal 5:22). They had experienced the gift of joy in the afflictions they suffered for their faith (1:6), and he had been made joyful by them (3:9).

(2) *'pray constantly.'* This is the third use of *'constantly'* in this letter, and all are connected with prayer. The others occur when Paul is describing his own constant gratitude to God (1:2; 2:13). Again, although he never repeats this command exactly, passages like Rom 12:12, Eph 6:18 and Col 4:2 as well as Lk 18:1 state that constant prayer is a quality of christian life. Paul never treats prayer extensively but mentions it briefly in most of his letters to the churches —either to tell them that he is praying for them or to urge them to pray. He offers his own actions in this area as a model for them.

(3) *'give thanks in all circumstances.'* Paul begins most of his letters with a thanksgiving prayer (cf. 1:2; 2:13) and often expresses thanks, but the closest parallel to this command is in the liturgical description of the community in Eph 5:20. No object of the verb is expressed, but God is to be understood, for he is the source of all goods that merit thanks.

The *'this'* of the next phrase (v.18) refers back to all three commands. In other words, *'the will of God in Jesus Christ'* is that they lead a life of constant joy, prayer and thanksgiving. Earlier Paul called their sanctification *'the will of God'* (4:3). Ordinarily when he speaks of *the will of God,'* Paul refers to God's saving plan for them in Christ, who reveals what God wants of them. Since their lives are rooted in *'the will of God,'* christian ethics is not limited to human horizons. Earthly history is only one aspect of the destiny that God offers to mortals *'in Christ Jesus.'* The christian understanding of grace is that with the revelation of his will God supplies mortals with the help they need to achieve the destiny he gives them. As Paul shows here, grace goes not eliminate human effort but empowers it. The response to grace can also be called *'the will of God.'*

In his final pieces of advice to the Thessalonians Paul reflects on problems arising from the charismatic element there. Charisms, or special spiritual manifestations of the Spirit's presence, often proved a two-edged sword in a church. On the one hand, they attracted persons to join the community. They fortified converts to accept the moral demands of christian conduct and to resist pressures and temptations. On the other hand, charismatic persons often took over a group and appeared to be overbearing. In this context Paul is warning against the danger of breaking into factions and of evaluating spiritual gifts by human prudence and convenience. Such a situation calls for discernment, which is one of the gifts of the Spirit needed to keep unity in Christ (cf. 1 Cor 12:10). Paul's basic attitude is to allow the charismatics freedom: *'do not quench the Spirit.'*

His pieces of advice show them how to translate this attitude into practice. The warning, *'do not despise prophecy,'* shows the direction of Paul's thought. Those who did not have this charism could resent either the honor paid to prophets or their power over community direction. The role of these christian prophets was not to predict future events but to declare God's will in the here and now. This gift was not confined to Jewish-christian circles. So outside forces may have been at work in its exercise at Thessalonica. If, as I mentioned in dealing with 4:15, the *'word of the Lord'* was a prophetic utterance, early christian prophets played an influential role in developing tradition. It is not surprising then that Paul gives extended advice about prophecy in 1 Cor 14.

Paul knows that individual prophets can be deceived (cf. 1 Cor 14:32; 2 Thess 2:2). So here he adds a warning, *'test everything; hold fast what is good.'* He had told them earlier that God *'tests our hearts'* (2:4). The term Paul uses for *'good'* is "the beautiful," the Greek expression of the aesthetic ideal, in contrast to the emphasis on moral goodness in verse 15. Perhaps Paul uses the aesthetical term for the *'good'* to which they are to hold fast because he speaks about the tradition that apostles hand on to new communities. Apostolic preaching enables future believers to experience the beauty of the Holy Spirit. As the apostles die, tradition becomes more significant in the church's life.

Paul closes this series of exhortations and warnings with the universal negative prohibition that grounds all moral activity, *'abstain from every form of evil.'* The word *'abstain'* belongs to the same root as *'hold fast'* in the previous sentence, so that a play on words results. An English equivalent might be, "Hold off from every expression of evil." This is an important admonition, especially for radical enthusiasts who may feel they are subject to no restraints. If *'form'* is to be taken as the various manifestations of self-deception brought on by the evil spirit (cf. 5:5), Paul's very way of expressing this principle points to the charismatic nature of the christian life as a whole. In his excellent reflections on Paul's letters to the Thessalonians, L. M. Dewailly devotes several pages to the question of evil in the community (pp. 110-116).

BLESSINGS, GREETINGS, INSTRUCTIONS.
1 Thess 5:23-27.

> [23]May the God of peace himself sanctify you wholly; and may your spirit and soul and body be kept sound and

blameless at the coming of our Lord Jesus Christ. [24]He who calls you is faithful, and he will do it.

[25]Brethren, pray for us.

[26]Greet all the brethren with a holy kiss.

[27]I adjure you by the Lord that this letter be read to all the brethren.

Paul closes this letter with a solemn invocation on behalf of the community in the form of a double petition. As he gathers himself in prayer Paul seems to be carried away and his words shift direction when he passes from the first to the second petition. As a result more than one interpretation is possible, and this verse continues to cause commentators problems. The RSV sees two parallel requests: (1) that God may satisfy them completely; (2) that their whole being—spirit, body and soul—may be preserved *'blameless'* for Christ's return.

In the opening petition, *'may the God of peace himself,'* the *'himself'* stands emphatically first in Greek. Thus Paul affirms that only God can achieve the holiness he has been exhorting them to pursue. Paul uses the title *'God of peace'* again in Rom 15:33; 16:20; 2 Cor 13:11 and Phil 4:9 (cf. 1 Cor 14:33), always in the context of a petition. This pattern, as well as the fact that it is in Semitic style, points to a liturgical origin. By Paul's time it was a stereotyped phrase, but what was its original meaning? It apparently celebrated God as the ultimate source and giver of all *shalom,* the healing and effective blessings needed for human wholeness. Paul's prayer is that God will *'sanctify'* them *'wholly,'* that is, on every level of existence—a word found in the bible only here. He had previously asserted that God called them to holiness and gave them his Holy Spirit (4:7-8). The Holy Spirit is the gift through which God brings about the transformation called sanctification, which is the first step of salvation in Christ. This petition then once more reminds them that holiness is a gift.

Rather than being parallel to the first prayer, the second petition seems to specify that request. In technical terms, the *'and'* is not coordinate but epexegetical or explanatory.

In Greek the prayer begins with the adjective *'sound'* and then lists the areas to be made sound, *'spirit and soul and body.'* This is the only time Paul brings these three items together as component elements of human beings. Elsewhere he speaks only of two elements: body and soul (1 Cor 5:3-5) or flesh and spirit (2 Cor 7:1). This anomaly still divides commentators as to its meaning in terms of Paul's anthropology. Pagan Greek writers gave body, soul and mind as components of human nature. Paul's viewpoint is not like theirs but flows from the biblical tradition of God as creator and savior. Hence, Paul's *'spirit'* is not equivalent to their mind.

He uses the term *'spirit'* flexibly to express a wide range of reality, extending all the way from the Holy Spirit as being what later theology calls the third person of the trinity. By extension *'spirit'* also refers to his indwelling in believers and to the effects he produces in them. This meaning blends with their ability to respond to the activity of the Holy Spirit. So Paul calls one who lives under the influence of the Spirit a *'spiritual'* person. Only the context makes it possible to determine the area of meaning covered by the term *'spirit.'* Its importance in Paul's letters testifies to the biblical insistence of the supremacy of the nonmaterial over the material element of human existence. The aim of this rhetorical plea is to support the members of the community in their quest for holiness by encouraging them to remain *'blameless'* until final judgment. Paul does not conceive of their *'spirit'* as a separate entity but rather as their power to motivate themselves under the guidance of the Holy Spirit.

His prayer does not stop there. Faith penetrates into every level of human life so that *'body'* and *'soul'* will be *'blameless'* and *'kept sound.'* These two words are separated with *'sound'* coming emphatically first in the prayer. But Paul then shifts into the passive voice making God the unexpressed agent by whom the are *'kept'* ready for Christ's return. The *'soul'* is the principle of physical life and all the activities that humans share with other living animals. Paul sees the *'body'* also as blessed and good; but in the lax atmosphere of hellenistic paganism it must be disciplined (cf. 4:1-9). The passage then does not offer significant help in clarifying Paul's anthropology.

The term for *'coming' (parousia)* is the presence of the glorified Jesus mentioned in 2:19; 3:13 and 4:15—one of the major concerns of both letters to the Thessalonians. Since they will share fully with every part of their being in the Lord's glory, Paul's petition acts as an exhortation to prepare for this *'coming'* and serves to give all these final exhortations an eschatological thrust. This is the twenty-second mention of Jesus as *'Lord'* in this short letter—a strong reminder that the power to remain holy comes from their faith in the promises of God and their hope in sharing in the victory of Jesus.

Paul explicitly refers to this basis of salvation at the end of this double petition when he reminds the Thessalonians that *'he who calls'* will bring about their triumph. The term *'call'* is a biblical idiom to express God's choosing a person or group for salvation. Paul's sense of having been called by God grounds his firm hope that bursts forth in his letters. *'He who calls'* is the Father, whose plan of salvation underlies not only this letter but all of Paul's writings (cf. 2:12; Rom. 9:12; Gal 5:8). In calling God *'faithful'* Paul is not referring to his good intentions but to his effective power to bring his promises to fulfilment. The same fidelity is attributed to Christ in 2 Thess 3:3. The fact that his hearers have been called is already a display of God's fidelity.

Once more Paul expresses his esteem for them by asking for the support of their prayers. He introduces this request by addressing them as *'brethren'* for the fourteenth time. Paul thus ends as he began—by placing himself on the same level as they are on in respect to salvation. Every believer receives it as gift and needs the support of others in keeping open to God's grace. The prayer is made in the present imperative, which has the note of continuing. A more faithful translation would be, "Keep praying for us also." This plea reinforces Paul's gentle attitude that he has maintained throughout this letter. In his letters Paul seldom asks for prayers, only in 2 Thess 3:1; Rom 15:30; 2 Cor 1:11 and Col 4:3.

The *'holy kiss'* greeting is mentioned by Paul again in Rom 16:16; 1 Cor 16:20 and 2 Cor 13:12. The only other New Testament reference to this practice is the *'kiss of love'* in 1 Pt 5:14. It was a ceremony to celebrate ritually the intimate friendship existing in christian communities. Its origin and form are not known, but the practice did not exist in the Jewish synagogue. It quickly became linked to the Eucharist where it signified the mutual reconciliation demanded of all believers before seeking communion with Jesus. Here it is presented as a way to *'greet'* one another. Paul includes final greetings in all of his letters except Gal.

The next and final instruction of this letter is not typical of Paul. In fact, the compound verb translated *'adjure'* never appears elsewhere in the bible and is rare in secular Greek. It seems to mean, "I ask you to swear." To call upon the Lord Jesus in such a formal way to confirm an oath is also unusual. Paul knew that many members of the community could not read themselves. Evidently he was anxious that all of them hear it first hand to be reassured of his concern and to cut off any misrepresentation of his position. The form contrasts with the mild tone of the letter in which Paul has been extremely careful not to alienate anyone.

At this point Paul shifts for the third time to the singular (cf. 2:18; 3:5). Is this to give a greater intensity to Paul's plea? Or does he know that a group is resisting his authority? Or is it simply that Paul actually wrote this sentence himself and becomes more emphatic? Whatever the reason, the public reading of his letters played an important role in their being accepted into the official canon of scripture of the christian church. Especially in their liturgical reading they continue to instruct and prod church members to holiness.

FINAL BLESSING.
1 Thess 5:28.

[28]The grace of our Lord Jesus Christ be with you.

Paul never omits the final blessing, although it does not come last in the canonical form of Romans, which ends with a doxology (Rom 16:25-27). His final blessing takes the place of the greeting that closes secular letters of the time. As in the salutation, Paul developed a distinctly christian close, corresponding to his new form of salutation, *'grace and peace.'* The final blessing is more flexible and has several variations; this formula is repeated exactly only in Rom 16:20 and 1 Cor 16:23. But it always includes *'grace'* in the same full christian sense that is has in the opening salutation. This repetition produces an overarching "inclusion" for the letter, the figure of speech of beginning and ending a literary unit with the same word (cf. 3:1-5).

What is the relation between *'grace'* and *'our Lord Jesus Christ'?* God the Father is the ultimate source of *'grace.'* In his role as *'Lord'* Jesus is the first recipient of this divine favor and its prime communicator through the Holy Spirit. In that sense *'our Lord Jesus Christ'* can be called God's grace. The life of grace depends on faith in him, for it is a sharing in his loyalty, power and abiding presence. Thus the final blessing is a prayer that the Thessalonians may experience the vision and dedication of the risen Jesus so that they will achieve the faith, love and hope Paul has been discussing with them and urging them to nourish in and among themselves. When they arrive *'with the Lord'* (4:17), they will know what his *'grace'* is.

2 THESSALONIANS

2 Thessalonians

GREETINGS TO THE COMMUNITY.
2 Thess 1:1-2.

> **1** Paul, Silvanus, and Timothy,
> To the church of the Thessalonians in God our Father and the Lord Jesus Christ:
> ²Grace to you and peace from God the Father and the Lord Jesus Christ.

THE GREETING is slightly longer than that of the first letter; it adds a word and a phrase. The word added is *'our'* to *'Father'* and the phrase added is *'from God the Father and the Lord Jesus Christ.'*

Paul used the phrase *'our Father'* in 1 Thess 3:11, 13, but in both cases the phrase is *'God and our Father,'* that is, he adds *'and'* before *'Father'* (cf. also Gal 1:3,4). The phrase *'God our Father'* occurs later in this letter but with the article before *'God'* (2:16). The addition of *'our'* to the designation of God as *'Father'* gives a more personal character to his relationship to believers. He is *'God'* of all but *'Father'* in a special way only to those born into Christ by faith. The fatherhood that Paul speaks about is that transcendent relationship established in the risen Jesus Christ through grace, which effects a new creation into divine life. The *'our'* also joins the senders *'Paul, Silvanus, and Timothy'* to the recipients in a closer bond. Both are equal as children of the same saving God and enjoy a unity that gives meaning to any particular role they enjoy in the community of believers.

Thus Paul begins this letter with the same attitude of gentleness and reverence that permeated his first letter to the Thessalonians. He immediately adds his customary opening blessing. By invoking the divine names he manifests his authority for what he is going to communicate. His message comes *'from'* God and Jesus in glory. An additional impact of such a repetition is that Paul has linked the Father and the Lord Jesus together in two prepositional phrases governed by *'in'* and *'from.'* This close bond makes them at least functionally equal with respect to the growth of the community. Together they are the sphere in which believers dwell and the common source of blessings for the community. That Christ can give these blessings as well as the Father is a strong affirmation that he enjoys all divine prerogatives fully.

What I wrote earlier about the salutation of the first letter covers any needed commentary on these verses. Paul's awareness of the unique relationship of Jesus to the Father shows that the basis for later trinitarian theology in the church has deep roots in the earliest stages of christian tradition.

THANKSGIVING FOR THEIR LOYALTY.
2 Thess 1:3-4.

> [3]We are bound to give thanks to God always for you, brethren, as is fitting, because your faith is growing abundantly, and the love of every one of you for one another is increasing. [4]Therefore we ourselves boast of you in the churches of God for your steadfastness and faith in all your persecutions and in the afflictions which you are enduring.

These two verses are actually only the beginning of the "thanksgiving" element of this letter, but they are better discussed separately because of the high emotional outpouring that takes over in verse 5. The thanksgiving proper, which extends through verse 10, is a single sentence. Paul's sentences tend to become longer as his emotions soar. Modern editors usually break these complicated outpourings into shorter sentences—as the RSV has done here—to provide a clear translation for modern readers.

As long as modern readers are aware of the flow of discourse, they can still experience the impact of Paul's message without being distracted by complicated syntax. Because of the volatile nature of the problems Paul has to deal with in this letter, he includes a special reaction in the second part of this opening thanksgiving (vv.5-10). Then he closes this part of the letter with a short prayer (vv.11-12).

In these opening verses of the thanksgiving Paul continues the same gentle concern for the Thessalonians that marked his previous letter. His preoccupations remain basically the same as he starts to move into the particular concern that prompted this letter, namely, questions about Christ's return.

This thanksgiving starts with a phrase repeated below (2:13) but never found in any other Pauline thanksgiving, *'we are bound to give thanks.'* Elsewhere Paul simply prays, *'we give thanks.'* This change in style seems to turn this thanksgiving from a real prayer into a reflection on prayer that Paul should offer as an apostle. Actually, however, he is borrowing a formula from Jewish liturgical prayer, as parallels in Philo and the repetition below witness. Roger D. Aus suggests that the community's situation of suffering prompted Paul to use the formula here.

The plural form throughout this letter is an act of politeness rather than an indication that the other missionaries were co-authors. Silvanus and Timothy are included out of courtesy for their apostolic activity, but responsibility for the message is Paul's alone. He is doing what he is *'bound'* to do as an apostle of Jesus Christ.

He continues his practice of inserting frequently into his letters the personal address *'brethren'*—seven times compared with 14 times in the first letter. But this is the only time that Paul addresses his recipients directly in an opening thanksgiving, a feature that could also be influenced by the liturgical nature of the formula. He is careful to keep open the channels of communication so that they can hear his message. Yet, in general, in this letter, Paul is not so effusive in inserting elements of phatic communion, that is, those personal features whose role is simply to keep communication open with his readers.

He seems more intent upon eliminating misunderstanding about the subject of their belief than in his earlier letter and insists that they eliminate abuses in their lifestyle. This eagerness could be a sign that he looks upon them as more mature now and capable of managing the situation *'as it is fitting'* for a community that has endured suffering for the Lord. The adjective *'fitting'* is rare in Paul, only four times in letters to the churches. It comes from the same root as the verb in the prayer below that is translated as *'worthy'* (1:11).

The subject of this thanksgiving is substantially the same as that of the first letter: their *'faith,'* mutual *'love'* and *'steadfastness.'* Perhaps "of hope" is to be understood with this final word (cf. 1 Thess 1:3). Now, however, Paul is even more enthusiastic about the community because they are practicing these qualities. Their faith is *'growing abundantly.'* This verb, a rare compound not found elsewhere in the bible, is equivalent to an English expression like "super-fruitful." Paul employs several words compounded with the prefix meaning "super," some of which are unique in the bible.

Paul gives an even fuller description of what merits his thanksgiving in their exercise of mutual *'love,'* namely, that it *'is increasing'* in the case of *'everyone of you for one another.'* This elaborate phrase, however, is evidently an exaggeration in light of the type of advice that he has to give them later in this letter and in his prayer that God may increase both their *'love'* and *'steadfastness'* (cf. 3:5). Paul also prayed for an *'increase'* of mutual love in his earlier letter (1 Thess 3:12).

This subtle intertwining of vocabulary from 1 Thess into this letter figures prominently in the controversy about the authenticity of 2 Thess. Those who deny that Paul is its author see this apparent imitation as the sign of a late forger. Those who hold the letter as authentic remark that similarities are the result of reflex activity in Paul's memory as it calls back expressions he used a few months earlier. However, as St. John Chrysostom comments on Paul's use of the term *'steadfastness,'* the letters could not be too close together because this word implies a long time lapse to prove their endurance.

At this point in the thanksgiving Paul becomes disturbed about the conditions that provoked this letter and goes off on a tangent. As he becomes emotional his mind rushes ahead and the result is an anacoluthon, or shift of grammatical construction within the sentence. The RSV reflects this lack of continuity in thought by starting a new sentence at verse 4 with *'Therefore'* and a finite verb. The Greek text has a subordinate construction indicating result: the conjunction *hoste* plus an infinitive. Paul skips over part of his reasoning process as he explains why it is fitting for him to be so grateful to God. He comes to the final result, namely, he has been able to *'boast'* in other communities about *'your steadfastness and faith in all your persecutions'* and other *'afflictions.'* In contrast to the pejorative sense of *'boast'* in Jewish literature, Paul frequently uses this expression in the sense of having an authentic religious experience (cf. 1 Thess 2:19).

Earlier he told them that communities throughout Achaia had heard of their faith (1 Thess 1:9). This repeated emphasis on the outstanding quality of their faith is another reason why some commentators favor a later date for both of these letters, but their arguments are not conclusive. How would Paul do this boasting? Either by letter (cf. 2 Cor 8:1) or by word of mouth. Nothing in Paul's other letters or in the rest of the New Testament singles out the Thessalonian christians for their *'steadfastness and faith.'* In fact, this is the only place in Paul where these two qualities are so closely linked. The *'and'* is apparently epexegetical or explanatory. Their *'steadfastness,'* which is an expression of their hope in sharing in Christ's return, is itself God's gift and the ultimate root of their faithful response to God's call. Because they trust in God's power to give them victory over their present *'persecutions'* and afflictions (cf. 1 Thess 1:6; 3:3), they are able to bear witness to their call to salvation. This is Paul's first mention of *'persecutions'* and he does not elaborate. So modern readers are left without further information about the situation.

This stringing out of prepositional phrases one after another is a frequent practice in Paul—a feature of his style that at times makes understanding difficult and translation even more so. No wonder the RSV cuts this sentence short and begins a new one with the description of the final judgment (v.5). This form of description flows out of Paul's eagerness to encourage the community and to prepare its members for the return of Jesus. From these reflections arises the prayer that will round out this thanksgiving. As usual, the entire passage introduces the subjects that Paul will discuss in this letter: faith, the nature of Christ's return and true christian lifestyle.

AN OUTPOURING ABOUT FINAL JUDGMENT. 2 Thess 1:5-10.

> [5]This is evidence of the righteous judgment of God, that you may be made worthy of the kingdom of God, for which you are suffering—[6]since indeed God deems it just to repay with affliction those who afflict you, [7]and to grant rest with us to you who are afflicted, when the Lord Jesus is revealed from heaven with his mighty angels in flaming fire, [8]inflicting vengeance upon those who do not know God and upon those who do not obey the gospel of our Lord Jesus. [9]They shall suffer the punishment of eternal destruction and exclusion from the presence of the Lord and from the glory of his might, [10]when he comes on that day to be glorified in his saints, and to be marveled at in all who have believed, because our testimony to you was believed.

The mention of their suffering triggers this outburst about the certainty and severity of final retribution. In the Greek text it begins abruptly with the noun *'evidence,'* placed in loose connection with the previously mentioned *'persecutions'* and *'sufferings.'* In fact, the phrase *'evidence of the righteous judgment of God'* stands in apposition to the whole last part of verse 4 about their *'steadfastness'* in *'sufferings.'* For modern readers this is an abrupt transition. But Paul's mentality is apocalyptically oriented, and he sees all human conduct as standing under the final authority of Jesus as Lord. In his first letter to them Paul reminded the Thessalonians that afflictions are the *'lot'* of believers (1 Thess 3:3). His goal in this letter is to deepen their understanding of the final judgment and thus prepare them to stand before Jesus blameless, as he had urged them once before (1 Thess 3:13).

The phrase *'righteous judgment'* is from the Old Testament and occurs in John's gospel, but never again in Paul. The last judgment is *'righteous'* in the sense that it has mysterious power to purify believers and thus prepare them for the *'kingdom of God'*—another infrequent phrase in Paul. For him it does not center on the present situation of God's revelation in Jesus as in the synoptic gospels but refers to the eschatological situation of eternal glory (cf. 1 Thess 2:12). These are the only times that Paul mentions the *'kingdom'* in these two letters.

The reference to the *'kingdom'* leads Paul to mention once more their present sufferings and the certainty that God will punish their persecutors. Just what kind of affliction he will send, Paul does not say. But from the flow of this passage it is clear that God's punishments on their enemies may look on the surface exactly like their own afflictions on behalf of the kingdom. Hence, the characteristic that distinguishes the sufferings of believers will be their faith and hope. These give assurance to believers that God will not abandon them. And so believers like Paul himself have *'evidence'* (word found in the bible only here) that God will intervene at the proper time to justify their trust in him (cf. Phil 1:28). The RSV omits the indication of the comparison in the Greek phrase that compares their sufferings to Paul's, namely, *'for which you* (also) *are enduring.'*

Those who enjoy this divine favor will eventually enjoy *'rest'* with Paul and the other missionaries at the return of Jesus, when he will be *'revealed from heaven with his mighty angels in flaming fire.'* This is an apocalyptic picture of the glorious return of Jesus. Paul here calls it a *'revelation.'* In his earlier letter he spoke of it as the *'parousia'* (cf. 1 Thess 2:19; 3:13; 4:15; 5:23), the term he uses below (2:1). Once more Paul describes it in terms of cosmic imagery (cf. 1 Thess 4:16-17), but now he stresses it as the moment of judgment.

In no other place does he speak of *'mighty angels,'* which in Greek is literally *'angels of might.'* The term "might" may be understood as a title for God so that the phrase means "God's angels." The image of fire comes from the Hebrew bible, which uses the same phrase *'in flaming fire'* in Ex 3:2 and Is 66:15. After giving this apocalyptic picture Paul explains the significance of the return of Jesus as the occasion for universal judgment. Although he attributes judgment to God in verse 5, it is administered by Jesus in verses 7-8, another example of how Paul attributes divine activities to Jesus as Lord.

Continuing to use phrases from scripture, Paul speaks of sinners as *'those who do not know God and do not obey'* the gospel of our Lord Jesus. Already Paul had described the pagans as those *'who do not know God'* (1 Thess 4:5), a phrase that goes back to Jer 10:24 and Ps 79:6 and appears in Gal 4:8. The same concept is expressed in popular philosophical language in Wis 13:1, which speaks of certain ones living "in ignorance of God" and being unable to recognize him as creator from his works. But Paul prefers the vocabulary of the apocalyptic tradition that was popular at Thessalonica. His preaching of the resurrection and return of Jesus must have encouraged some of the excesses that he now has to moderate.

In no way does Paul wish to lessen joyful expectation of Christ's return. But he wants to make the community conscious that it will have a twofold effect, both to reward and to punish. He also adds a specifically christian dimension to not knowing God, namely, sinners *'do not obey the gospel of our Lord Jesus.'* God offers a new self-manifestation in the coming of Jesus. His life, teaching, death and resurrection are revelations to humanity of God's saving will.

Paul used the term *'gospel'* six times in the earlier letter, three of these in the phrase *'gospel of God'* (1 Thess 2:2, 8, 9), that is, the concrete expression of the Father's plan of salvation. He called Timothy a servant of God in *'the gospel of Christ'* (1 Thess 3:3) as the one he sent to complete his instructions in how they were to identify with the mission of Jesus. Now he speaks of the *'gospel of our Lord Jesus,'* meaning that it is the pledge of Jesus' presence to believers as their support in present suffering. But Paul's stress is on the side of warning. One cannot *'know God,'* that is, worship him and relate to him in a saving way, except by obeying the Lord Jesus. The *'and'* between the two forms of conduct—not knowing God and not obeying the gospel—is an expression of absolute identity. The only way to worship the Father is to serve the Lord Jesus. Those who refuse to do so *'shall suffer the punishment of eternal destruction.'* Paul expresses himself in the ordinary secular Greek idiom of "pay the penalty," not found elsewhere in the New Testament.

Earlier Paul linked *'destruction'* to the *'day of the Lord'* (1 Thess 5:3). Hence, the *'eternal'* here refers to the specific kind of punishment linked to the time of Christ's return. The image of the day of the Lord is not explicit here but it seems to underlie this passage, which ends emphatically with the phrase *'on that day.'* This phrase comes at the end of verse 10 in Greek rather than at the beginning, as in RSV. Once more Paul links it to Jesus, who will assume the role that Yahweh played in the Hebrew bible. Phrases used by the prophet Isaiah to describe God are here applied to the effect of Christ's coming as judge upon sinners. They will be removed *'from the presence of the Lord and from the glory of his might'* (quoting Is 2:19). Isaiah was describing the day of the Lord, a time when Yahweh would punish Israel's sins. Apocalyptic writers took over this kind of language to describe God's final judgment. Paul adopts apocalyptic style but gives the role of judge to the risen Jesus.

The words *'and exclusion'* (v.9) are inserted by the RSV into the quotation but are not in the Greek text. They make Isaiah say that *'eternal destruction'* is *'exclusion from the presence of the Lord,'* as long as readers understand the *'and'* as explanatory and not as adding an additional punishment.

Paul becomes carried away by all of this imagery and expands it in oratorical phrasing modeled on the text of Isaiah and the Psalms to give a positive picture of the glorious return of Jesus as a world-transforming presence for the benefit of believers (v.10). The Lord will *'be glorified,'* that is, receive divine honor. This compound verb is found only in the biblical tradition, which speaks of God's *'glory'* as the external manifestation of his power (cf. v.9). Paul repeats this rare compound in the prayer below (v.12)—the only two appearances in the New Testament (cf. Ps 89:7).

Paul pictures this glorification as taking place *'in his saints,'* a phrase recalling his statement that the *'saints'* will be with the glorified Jesus at his parousia (1 Thess 3:13). The *'in'* of this phrase is equivalent to "by," in accordance with the Hebrew idiom. The term *'saints'* embraces the holy ones of both the Old and New Testaments. They glorify Christ by preferring him above all else and will lead his praise at his return. In glorifying Jesus they will also share forever in his glory, which is the communication of his power. This gift is the way God justifies their faith and perseverance. Extending the sense of the statement, St. John

Chrysostom comments that tribulation for the sake of Christ is glory.

All who have persevered in faith will *'marvel'* at the event of Christ's return. In this phrase Paul is not referring to a different group from the *'saints'* but reinforces the point he made in this earlier letter that both the living and the dead believers would share in Christ's glory forever (cf. 1 Thess 4:13-18). Physical death will offer no obstacle to sharing in eternal life, which is the reward of those who believe, in contrast to the *'eternal destruction'* of their persecutors. By picturing Jesus as recipient of this glory, Paul affirms his divine status.

The syntax of Paul's outburst is irregular in Greek, but the RSV smoothes over the grammatical awkwardness to make clear that the necessary condition of sharing in Christ's glory is *'to have believed'* in his *'testimony.'* The repetition of the verb *'believe'* in verse 10 closes the outpouring by emphasizing the basis of eternal life. Faith is what makes the sufferings of christians bearable. Only at Christ's return will this faith reach its full growth. Paul began this thanksgiving with the mention of faith. By returning to it at the end of his vivid description of Christ's return he produces a literary inclusion that binds this thanksgiving into a tight unity.

With the completion of the circle Paul suddenly drops the topic and brings the thanksgiving to an abrupt close. He has not only introduced his recipients to the topic that he will develop but has started to create the mood they will need to hear this message. In general, the erratic nature of this passage is a strong argument for the authenticity of this letter. Surely a forger would have been more careful to produce a composition easier to follow. Paul's parenthetical way of speaking directly to the Thessalonians and of congratulating them for their growth is another example of his skill in using phatic communication, that is, in keeping lines of communication open. He is constantly opening the channels of good will as he moves into correcting them and clarifying their misunderstandings about Christ's return.

PRAYER FOR THEIR GROWTH.
2 Thess 1:11-12.

> [11]To this end we always pray for you, that our God may make you worthy of his call, and may fulfil every good resolve and work of faith by his power, [12]so that the name of our Lord Jesus may be glorified in you, and you in him, according to the grace of our God and the Lord Jesus Christ.

As usually happens, Paul's opening thanksgiving ends with a petition that flows from the subject matter he treats. Its purpose is to increase their love for the gifts God has given them and to encourage them to open themselves to the instructions he is going to give them about the good news. This prayer is an integral part of the thanksgiving, as the opening phrase *'to this end'* shows. Paul gathers together into a real plea the courage they have displayed and the consolation he has received through them. In his earlier letter he had asked them to pray for him (1 Thess 5:25). Now he gives them an insight into the kind of prayer to offer.

He does not specify to whom he prays, but that can be surmised from the opening words of the thanksgiving (v.3). Paul prays to *'God,'* that is, the Father of Jesus Christ, because he is the ultimate source of grace and peace. The RSV does not translate an *'also'* at the opening of verse 11 and so misses a nuance in Paul's thought. He and his companions *(also)* pray *'to this end.'* That is, in addition to their preaching and community-building activities, the apostles do not neglect the special form of worship that wins God's grace. Prayer of petition is not a separate category in their lives, but they *'always pray'* for the Thessalonians just as they *'give thanks always'* for them (v.3; cf. 1 Thess 2:13).

Embodied in this petition is a theology of prayer. Paul knows that the life of faith operates out of the vision that God not only cares for his people but also wills that all members of the community constantly support one another. Paul's prayer celebrates this saving will and spells out two specific aspects of it:

(1) *'that our God may make you worthy of his call'*—a profound religious insight with many implications. Paul prays as one joined to the community by a common faith, as a fellow servant of *'our God.'* He prays out of an awareness that only God can give the ability to respond to his *'call,'* a word Paul reserves for God's saving activity. Their faith response arises out of God's initiative as their Father intervening in their lives. Within this *'call'* is power to respond, for it *'makes you worthy,'* that is, provides all the help that brought them to their present state of growth and will insure their perseverance. The life of faith is a journey; so they need to be receptive to its ever-growing demands. This prayer serves both to encourage and warn this young community. It echoes Paul's wish that they *'lead a life worthy of God who calls'* them to glory (1 Thess 2:12) and looks to their present activity that Paul will touch upon later.

(2) that our God *'may fulfil every good resolve and work of faith by his power.'* This second part of the petition places emphasis on the human part of growth in faith. Paul prays that they will cooperate actively with God's *'call'* by their good will and by their *'work of faith,'* a phrase that appears in the opening thanksgiving of the earlier letter (1 Thess 1:3). The *'and'* between these two phrases is not a simple coordinating conjunction. Rather it specifies that *'every good resolve'* comes as a gift of the faith that is the primary source of eternal life. Through their cooperation with grace God sets up the dynamism of spiritual growth *'by his power'* at work in them individually and collectively. Grace does not eliminate human responsibility but makes cooperation possible. Their manner of living is the witness to pagans in general and to their persecutors in particular that God's *'power'* is at work in them.

The terminology Paul uses in this prayer to express this truth is unusual. The phrase translated *'good resolve'* consists of two nouns found almost exclusively in the bible. They are linked in the Hebrew idiom which reads literally "good will of goodness," which Paul calls a fruit of the Spirit in Gal 5:22. The goal of this prayer is to communicate Paul's sense of how important God's final judgment through Jesus is and how carefully they should prepare for it. He urges them to live *'worthy'* of their dignity as children of God who alone empowers them to overcome persecutions and difficulties. Their witness is an aspect of their *'call'* in God's plan. So Paul closes this short petition with a statement of God's purpose in calling them and enriching them with all his gifts. It is so that *'the name of our Lord Jesus may be glorified'* among them and by them. Paul repeats the unusual compound of *'glorified'* used above (v.10, alluding to Is 66:5). All creation glorifies the Father through the exaltation of the *'Lord Jesus Christ.'*

Paul uses a biblical idiom when he prays that the *'name of the Lord'*—rather than simply the risen Jesus—be *'glorified.'* The *'name'* represents the public manifestation of God for the benefit of his people. By applying this idiom to *'our Lord Jesus,'* Paul again implies his divine power in the Father's plan. He goes even further now by including their worship of Jesus as the very goal of that plan. This worship does not remain an external rite but becomes a mutual interaction. They glorify Jesus as Lord by praying to him; he in turn glorifies them by bringing them to share in his victory. Paul represents this state as the goal of creation in his concluding phrase, *'according to the grace of our God . . .'.* We would expect him to stop there and so attribute this result exclusively to the Father, as he does both in the first part of this prayer (v.11) and in the beginning of the entire thanksgiving (v.3). Instead he continues and attributes this grace also to *'the Lord Jesus,'* using a solemn title already established in the church.

Paul associates the glorified Jesus on an equal level with the Father as giver of the grace that brings believers to their salvation. This prayer thus becomes a strong affirmation that he sees an equality between Father and Son in the work of saving humans. Although Paul did not address Jesus explicitly at the beginning of this prayer, he ends by attributing divine power to the *'Lord Jesus Christ'* in a way that does not deprive the Father of special initiative in creation and salvation. The addition of this final phrase throws the flow of the sentence off somewhat because it states that the grace of Jesus glorifies his name; but this inbalance illustrates the paradox that Jesus is both agent and channel of grace.

A REMINDER THAT THE DAY OF THE LORD HAS NOT ARRIVED.
2 Thess 2:1-2.

> **2** Now concerning the coming of our Lord Jesus Christ and our assembling to meet him, we beg you, brethren, [2]not to be quickly shaken in mind or excited, either by spirit or by word, or by letter purporting to be from us, to the effect that the day of the Lord has come.

Paul now takes up one of the two major problems that prompted this letter. In a carefully constructed periodic sentence that leads up to the major point, he begs them not to be deceived concerning *'the day of the Lord'*— a subject he had dealt with in 1 Thess 5:1-5. Evidently his teaching was misunderstood or others were misrepresenting him, for he is forced to reopen the question. He does this with great respect for their feelings by inserting several elements of phatic communication to minimize any misunderstanding. Thus he puts his advice in the form of a request, *'we beg you,'* and addresses them as *'brethren.'* He used the verb *'beg'* two times in his earlier letter to them (1 Thess 4:1; 5:12) so that three out of its four Pauline occurrences are in the Thessalonian correspondence.

His concern here is not primarily about *'the coming of our Lord Jesus Christ'* itself. He emphatically repeats the full title found in the prayer above (1:12). Although he is speaking about Jesus' glorious return or parousia (cf. 1 Thess 2:19; 3:13; 4:15; 5:23), he now treats it with respect to *'our assembling to meet him.'* The term for *'assembling'* is from the same root as synagogue, the Jewish meeting place. Paul is dealing with belief in the transforming coming of Jesus to meet both deceased and living believers *'in the air'* (cf. 1 Thess 4:17).

Some of the radical enthusiasts of the Thessalonian church were presenting a theory that *'the day of the Lord'* had already arrived. In technical language they proclaimed over-realized eschatology. This is part of the complicated question of the coming of the final age according to the writers of New Testament works. On the one hand, 1 Cor 10:11 speaks of the end of the ages as having come, but 2 Tim 3:1 says that the last days are still to come.

The practical consequence of the theory about over-realized eschatology was that the community at Thessalonica was upset. No doubt Timothy had stayed with them for a period of time after delivering Paul's first letter. He could have found out about this speculation and told Paul after his return to Corinth where Paul was still preaching. Paul would not have delayed long in addressing this grave problem. This sequence of events points to the probable date of this letter, that is, in 51 A. D., within six months of Paul's first letter.

The effect of this speculation was to leave members of the community *'shaken in mind or excited.'* The verb *'shake'* appears only here in Paul but occurs in apocalyptic passages dealing with cosmic upheaval (cf. Mt 24:29; Lk 21:26). The RSV phrase *'shaken in mind'* is not idiomatic English. The Greek text means that they have lost composure. It is less forceful than the companion verb translated as *'excited,'* a word used in Jesus' apocalyptic discourse to calm his disciples (cf. Mt 24:6; Mk 13:7).

Paul lists three sources that have been blamed as causes for the spread of the disturbing speculation about *'the day of the Lord,'* namely: (1) *'by spirit.'* Rigaux thinks it is impossible to specify what *'spirit'* means here and leaves it vague as some action of the Holy Spirit. Possibly it means prophecies spoken by community members overwhelmed by an outpouring of *'spirit.'* *Today's English Version* specifies it as Paul's own prophetic teaching, thus making this source parallel with the two that follow. No consensus exists among commentators.

(2) *'by word.'* This probably refers to the teaching of preachers who came into the community. Some regard it as a misunderstanding of Paul's own preaching. Often it is interpreted in relation to the next source.

(3) *'by letter purporting to be from us,'* that is, Paul. The RSV translation implies that the letter had been falsely attributed to Paul. But the Greek text can also be interpreted to say, "on the basis of its being from me," that is, Paul complains that some are using his letter incorrectly. Arguing from this understanding of the text, Robert Jewett concludes that the *'word'* and *'letter'* that served as the basis for the theories that Paul here rejects were his own preaching and the earlier letter to them. He points out passages in 1 Thess that could be misunderstood by radical enthusiasts, for example, 1 Thess 2:16, 18; 3:13; 5:1-10. He concludes that Paul was shocked when he heard how his teaching was being misunderstood and quickly wrote this letter to correct their misrepresentations.

On the basis of that interpretation Paul describes his own letter as *'purporting to be from us'* because he does not recognize his ideas in these false theories and repudiates them. Paul does not deal any further with these misrepresentations but abruptly cuts short his warnings about their ideas on *'the day of the Lord.'* He prefers to turn immediately to aspects of the false teachings that are disturbing the community.

RESTRAINING THE OPPRESSOR.
2 Thess 2:3-12.

> [3]Let no one deceive you in any way; for that day will not come, unless the rebellion comes first, and the man of lawlessness [a] is revealed, the son of perdition, [4]who

opposes and exalts himself against every so-called god or object of worship, so that he takes his seat in the temple of God, proclaiming himself to be God. [5]Do you not remember that when I was still with you I told you this? [6]And you know what is restraining him now so that he may be revealed in his time. [7]For the mystery of lawlessness is already at work; only he who now restrains it will to so until he is out of the way. [8]And then the lawless one will be revealed, and the Lord Jesus will slay him with the breath of his mouth and destroy him by his appearing and his coming. [9]The coming of the lawless one by the activity of Satan will be with all power and with pretended signs and wonders, [10]and with all wicked deception for those who are to perish, because they refused to love the truth and so be saved. [11]Therefore God sends upon them a strong delusion, to make them believe what is false, [12]so that all may be condemned who did not believe the truth but had pleasure in unrighteousness.

[a]Other ancient authorities read *sin*

These verses contain the most difficult points of the two letters to the Thessalonians. They introduce material not found in any other Pauline letter. In particular those commentators who consider 2 Thess as non-Pauline see the attitude toward the eschaton or final stage of God's plan presented here as contradicting what Paul teaches about the imminent return of Jesus. For that reason these verses provide their principal basis for seeing this letter as pseudepigraphical, that is, as the work of a forger assuming Paul's name to gain a hearing. It is important to follow the text carefully in order both to arrive at the true message of this difficult paragraph and to evaluate theories questioning the authenticity of the letter.

Paradoxically, one strong argument for holding that these verses were actually written by Paul is their irregular style. The sentence that starts in verse 3 breaks off at the end of verse 4 without being completed, thus creating an anacoluthon. A second anacoluthon, or shift of grammatical construction within the sentence, occurs in the middle of verse 7, which is also left incomplete. Such grammatical irregularities appear in Paul's letters, usually in passages of intense feeling or of complicated comparisons. If the author were not Paul but a forger seeking to introduce a new eschatology after Paul's death, would he be so careless in presenting a counterposition?

The following brief comments on these obscure verses conclude that they are truly from Paul and deal with an obscure dimension of his early eschatological teaching. He presents two facts to show that *'the day of the Lord'* has not yet arrived: (1) the *'rebellion'* must come first, and (2) *'the man of lawlessness'*—or *'of sin'* according to the RSV note—must be *'revealed'* first. This man will eventually establish himself *'in the temple of God, proclaiming himself to be God.'* Fathers of the church like St. John Chrysostom and other commentators identify this man with the antichrist, but Paul does not say that.

The RSV has eliminated Paul's anacoluthon by completing the opening sentence with a phrase not found in Greek, *'that day will not come.'* Some addition is needed and this is a phrase that Paul himself could have easily omitted in the excitement of responding to the problem created by the false theory. The *'rebellion'* referred to is of a religious nature. Its Greek form—related to the word "apostasy"—is found again in the New Testament only in Acts 21:21. Although Paul never refers to this event again, the great apocalyptic sermon of Jesus predicted the rise of false christs and false prophets before the return of the Son of Man (cf. Mt 24:24; also 1 Jn 2:18).

Who is this apparently personal agent of evil who must arise before *'the day of the Lord'?* Paul describes him in several phrases:

(1) *'the man of lawlessness.'* Jesus' apocalyptic discourse points to *'lawlessness'* as a sign of the last days (Mt 24:12).

(2) *'the son of perdition.'* This is an idiomatic expression found in Semitic languages to designate one destined to be destroyed (cf. Jn 17:12, of Judas; compare the "sons of

light" in 1 Thess 5:5). The same root appears below of those who are to *'perish'* (v. 10).

(3) one *'who opposes and exalts himself against every so-called god or object of worship.'* This imagery comes from such apocalyptic pieces as Ez 28:2 and Dan 11:36, which became linked with the historical profanation of the temple of Jerusalem in the second century B.C. With this phrase Paul comes closest to portraying the figure of the antichrist that appears in later New Testament writers. Paul himself never mentions this person elsewhere. Yet he continues with an expression of astonishment, *'Do you not remember that when I was still with you I told you this?'* Chrysostom interprets this as an expression of confidence to soften their hearts before reproving them.

This question comes as a surprise because Paul obviously gave the Thessalonians the impression that they would all be alive at the triumphant return of Jesus (cf. 1 Thess 4:13-18). Paul now has to modify their expectations. Our difficulties in understanding this paragraph increase when Paul asserts that they *'know what is restraining'* this adversary. His surprise implies that he had encountered over-realized eschatology during his preaching at Thessalonica and showed why it was to be rejected. His omission of any reference to the problem elsewhere indicates that it did not surface again in this same form. If that is so, historical circumstances rather than forgery explain the unique mention of this topic in Paul's letters to the churches.

Because the recipients knew what Paul was referring to by these expressions about *'what is restraining'*—referred to both in the neuter (v. 6) and the masculine (v. 7)—he does not have to elaborate. This vagueness has complicated matters for this commentators down through history. They did not have the knowledge available to Paul's original readers and have reached a variety of solutions in trying to identify this mysterious person or thing. None of the solutions, ancient or modern, is entirely satisfactory. The more frequent opinions identify the force restraining

the *'man of lawlessness'* as the Roman empire or the
emperor or christian preaching in general or Paul's
missionary activity in particular. E. Best gives a detailed
summary of the treatment of this figure in his commentary
(pp. 290-302).

In an original series of studies concerning this paragraph
Roger D. Aus points to the influence of Is 66 on Paul's
development. He concludes that *'he who now restrains'*
is God himself, but viewed as author of salvation history.
This is why Paul refers to him in the neuter also—to specify
that *'what is restraining'* is the dimension of God's saving
plan that includes preaching the gospel to the pagans. This
explanation is quite plausible if verses 5-7 are viewed as
an explanatory parenthesis. If these are seen as an aside to
involved members of the church, the whole paragraph
moves more smoothly and advances from present to future.

Yet, even with these and other suggested explanations,
it remains true that the text remains obscure to modern
readers who do not have a complete understanding of
the background. This paragraph is a good example of
the semantic principle that writers and speakers are less
careful grammatically and less explicit when they are
discussing topics familiar to participants of a heated inter-
change. In this case an added problem is present: the literary
form of the passage is apocalyptic, which moves in stylized
images rather than in logical progression. All efforts to
explain the text in purely conceptual terms will fail.

Failure to find further reference to this restraining force
elsewhere in Paul is not sufficient to reject this letter as
inauthentic. Even B. Rigaux, the most complete commentator on these early letters of Paul, speaks of these
verses "with hesitation" (p. 665). Given our present lack
of knowledge about the background, the best procedure
seems to be to do what Paul himself did and move into
the final part of the paragraph. One final word on the
term *'mystery'* is in order. Ordinarily Paul uses it in the
good sense of God's secret plan of salvation. But even the

'mystery of godlessness' benefits believers because it falls under the control of the plan of God as the one *'who now restrains it.'*

Beginning with verse 8 Paul explains what he means by the phrase *'in his time'* (v. 6), that is, the proper moment for the restraining force to be revealed. This will be the moment of the parousia or return of Jesus as victor over his cosmic adversary. Paul continues to describe this victory of Jesus in apocalyptic terms because the *'appearing'* and *'coming'* of Jesus—two terms for the same reality—is an event that shakes the cosmos. Alluding to the Davidic heir (cf. Is 11:4), Paul pictures Jesus as the one who will *'slay'* this *'lawless one'* with *'the breath of his mouth.'*

Using the basic technique of Hebrew poetry, that is, the style called parallelism, Paul describes this return of Jesus in the imagery of the biblical holy war. Jesus will confront *'the lawless one,'* who also has his parousia or *'coming,'* a term Paul elsewhere reserves for the final victory of the risen Jesus. This vocabulary alerts the Thessalonians about how serious their great confrontation will be. It is the final conflict between *'the Lord Jesus'* and *'Satan'* (cf. 1 Thess 2:18), whose *'all power'* is capable of producing *'pretended signs and wonders'* (cf. Mt 24:24). The Greek text reads "signs and wonders of falsehood," that is, activities that both manifest Satan's deceit and have power to mislead humans. They will lead to destruction those *'who are to perish,'* a stereotyped expression for hardened sinners (cf. 1 Cor 1:18). To this description of sinners Paul adds a phrase at the end of verse 10 to affirm that their damnation results from their own choice, *'because they refused to love the truth'* that could save them. This unusual phrase calls attention to the need of believers to nourish themselves on the message of the good news that has power to communicate salvation.

In the case of those who maliciously refuse its grace, God *'sends upon them a strong delusion.'* Again Paul uses a Semitic idiom, which is literally "the activity of

error" (cf. 1 Thess 2:3), the antithesis of *'to love the truth.'*
As is usual in Semitic thought God is pictured as the cause
of making them *'believe what is false.'* Paul imitates the
prophetic approach that pictures sin as carrying destruction
within itself. Punishment is part of an inexorable process.
As the one who supports all creation, God is represented
as the ultimate cause of human malice as well as the source
of the resulting punishment.

In the final sentence of this paragraph Paul returns to
more sober christian vocabulary to identify sinners as
those who *'did not believe the truth.'* His use of the aorist
participle of the verb *'believe'* shows that he is not talking
in general terms but pinpoints the moment of fundamental
option, making the choice to embrace the good news. Those
who *'had pleasure in unrighteousness'* will *'be condemned'*
for not accepting and living out God's saving *'truth.'*

OUTBURST OF THANKS AND ENCOURAGEMENT.
2 Thess 2:13-15.

> [13]But we are bound to give thanks to God always for
> you, brethren beloved by the Lord, because God chose
> you from the beginning[b] to be saved through sanctifi-
> cation by the Spirit[c] and belief in the truth. [14]To this
> he called you through our gospel, so that you may obtain
> the glory of our Lord Jesus Christ. [15]So then, brethren,
> stand firm and hold to the traditions which you were
> taught by us, either by word of mouth or by letter.

> [b]Other ancient authorities read *as first converts.*
> [c]Or *of spirit.*

In this short section Paul radically shifts direction. In
the form of a prayer he summarizes what he has already
said and anticipates the encouragement he will spell out
in detail later in the letter. Instead of simply stating their
advantages as believers, Paul breaks into a second thanksgiving prayer. He begins by repeating the opening words

of the liturgical thanksgiving of this letter, *'we are bound to give thanks to God always for you'* (cf. 1:3). He expands this prayer by an elaborate form of address similar to the salutation of the earlier letter, *'brethren beloved by the Lord'* (cf. 1 Thess 1:4). But here he substitutes the term *'Lord,'* meaning the risen Jesus, for *'God,'* namely, the Father.

This long address is a form of phatic communication that helps prepare them to hear the strong advice he is soon going to give them. This reminder that their new dignity is something given by God's choice of them to be believers is an implicit appeal for fidelity in the trials they must face. The RSV accepts the reading *'from the begining,'* but many commentators prefer to follow the manuscripts that read, "God chose you *as the first fruits* unto salvation." This is the choice of the RSV note, which translates, *'as the first converts to be saved.'* As one of the first groups in Europe to be converted principally from paganism, the Thessalonians should be grateful for all that Paul has just recalled, especially if what restrains *'the mystery of lawlessness'* (2:7) is God's plan for the preaching of the gospel throughout the world.

Paul adds two essential conditions for salvation:

(1) *'sanctification by the Spirit.'* The Greek reads *'of spirit,'* as found in the RSV note. Theoretically this could refer to the human spirit, but the context favors the RSV text and interpretation that Paul refers to the activity of the Holy Spirit as the personal agent for human transformation. This is the third time the term *'spirit'* occurs in this chapter (vv. 2, 8 and 13). It is the clearest reference to the Holy Spirit, a title never found in this letter. Paul is brief here because he dealt with the effects of sanctification in 1 Thess 4:3-7. In both texts he refers to the activity of Father, Son and Spirit, but here Paul simply recalls to believers their responsibility to let the Holy Spirit operate in and through them for their transformation into children of God.

(2) *'belief in the truth.'* Again the Greek is less specific and says simply, "by faith of truth." A few verses earlier Paul spoke about the *'love of truth'* necessary for salvation (v. 10) and about those who *'did not believe the truth'* (v. 12). Now he urges them to render thanks to God for the great gifts of faith and love that open up eternal life to them.

The *'this'* at the beginning of verse 14 does not look back but forward to the goal of their calling, namely, to *'obtain the glory of our Lord Jesus Christ.'* Paul is using different words to affirm what he said in his earlier letter: God calls believers *'to obtain salvation through our Lord Jesus Christ'* (1 Thess 5:9). Salvation is sharing in the risen life or *'glory'* of the Lord Jesus. Being aware of this gift begets gratitude, which acts as a strong motivating force toward perseverance in their calling despite obstacles such as persecution (cf. 1:11-12). Paul's preaching, which he calls *'our gospel,'* is the channel God uses to communicate this life-giving truth.

He concludes this brief thanksgiving prayer with an appeal that they *'stand firm'* (cf. 1 Thess 3:8) in this *'gospel'* in whatever form they hear it from him, whether this be by oral preaching, *'word of mouth,'* or by writing, *'letter.'* His gospel embraces a wide range of conduct. He calls its content *'the traditions'* (cf. 1 Cor 11:2; Gal 1:14; Col 2:8; 2 Thess 3:6). They include liturgical and doctrinal guidance as well as moral activity. The phrase *'hold to the traditions'* occurs again in the New Testament only in a controversy between Jesus and his opponents, where Jesus is warning against human traditions (cf. Mk 7:3, 8). By using this phrase Paul acts as an apostle to affirm his right to impose a way of acting upon a community even by written communication.

The presence of this second thanksgiving in a position similar to the second one in 1 Thess 2:13-16 has been cited as a reason for seeing this letter as pseudo-Pauline, a forgery imitating the earlier letter. Yet this argument is far from decisive. In fact, this stylistic feature could also point to this letter as being an early composition of Paul who was still developing an appropriate format and still working out the shaping principle of an authoritative apostolic letter.

PRAYER FOR THE COMMUNITY.
2 Thess 2:16-17.

> [16]Now may our Lord Jesus Christ himself, and God our Father, who loved us and gave us eternal comfort and good hope through grace, [17]comfort your hearts and establish them in every good work and word.

As is customary in a Pauline thanksgiving, this one also ends in a prayer of petition. This petition resembles the one at the end of Paul's third thanksgiving in 1 Thess 3:11-13 but is shorter because of significant omissions. Both begin with the emphatic *'himself,'* which cannot come first in the English translation. Here, however, *'our Lord Jesus Christ'* is named before *'God our Father.'* This order, plus the placing of these two names in perfect parallel and linking them in a clause with the two verbs *'comfort'* and *'establish'*—both singular in the Greek—form a strong affirmation that Father and Son are equal partners in sanctifying humans. For Paul, the term God ordinarily means the Father, but here he makes this identification explicit.

The full title *'our Lord Jesus Christ'* is more frequent in the letters to the Thessalonians than in other Pauline writing (cf. 1 Thess 1:3; 5:9, 23, 28; 2 Thess 2:1, 14, 16; 3:18). These make up more than a third of times Paul uses the full title, but he employs other variations also. In the New Testament the full title appears also in Acts, James, 1 Pt, 2 Pt and Jude.

It could be argued that Paul means to limit the subject of the relative clauses, *'who loved us and gave us eternal comfort and good hope through grace,'* to the Father, and so mentions him after Jesus. In favor of that interpretation can be said that the participles in Greek are singular (cf. Rom 15:5; 2 Cor 1:3). Yet the main verbs of the sentence are singular and they certainly include Jesus. Also, Paul attributes the actions of loving us and giving hope to us to Jesus. The fact that both the main clause and the participles include the idea of *'comfort'* seems decisive in favor of including Jesus in the subject of both.

The participles are in the aorist form, pointing to a single past act. This means that Paul is not speaking about a series of successive actions. Rather he groups the entire support of the Father and Jesus into a single, definitive, saving intervention. This recalls what he stated above, namely, that God *'chose'* them (v.13). The suggestion in the Ellingworth-Nida volume that Paul is alluding to the death and resurrection of Jesus as the unique expression of God's love is plausible (cf. Gal 2:19-20). Chrysostom points out the importance of this prayer when he comments that souls are shaken when they are not fully persuaded that they are progressing toward a good goal.

Paul specifies that their *'comfort'* is *'eternal'* because, depite the trials the community is now undergoing. God is going to give them unending reward. This reward is the result of the *'good hope'* God has already given them *'through grace.'* Thus later theologians will say that grace is the beginning of glory. The Greek text says "in grace," a phrase Paul uses again only in Col 3:16 and 4:6.

Throughout this prayer Paul shows great economy of words, each of which invites reflection and response. When he prays that God may *'comfort your hearts,'* he is using *'heart'* in the wide meaning it has in Semitic anthropology as the seat of reflection and moral choice as well as source of emotions. When God *'comforts your hearts and establishes them,'* he is blessing their entire existence so that they may accomplish *'every good work and word.'* Paul places more value on the witness of living out the message than on talking about it. Good works flow from the grace that he also prayed for at the end of his opening thanksgiving (cf. 1:11-12).

A CALL FOR PRAYER.
2 Thess 3:1-5.

> **3** Finally, brethren, pray for us, that the word of the Lord may speed on and triumph, as it did among you, [2]and that we may be delivered from wicked and evil men; for not all have faith. [3]But the Lord is faithful; he will strengthen you and guard you from evil.[d] [4]And we have confidence in the Lord about you, that you are doing and will do the things which we command. [5]May the Lord direct your hearts to the love of God and to the steadfastness of Christ.
>
> [d]Or *the evil one.*

Paul still finds it difficult to tell other believers how to conduct themselves. Yet he must do so because he is founder of this community and some of its members are not conducting themselves according to the traditions he esteems as important for church life (cf. 2:15). For the third time since 2:13 he addresses them as *'brethren,'* gradually edging into the specific directions he must give by this exercise of phatic communication and by this extended call to prayer. This approach is more plausible in Paul than in a forger.

The request for prayers, which is a customary feature in some letters, comes earlier than usual (cf. 1 Thess 5:25). Paul still has an important point to cover. Because he will have to speak bluntly to them, he may have felt he was in a better position at this moment in the letter to show that he valued their support. The present imperative of this petition in Greek is stronger than the RSV's, *'pray for us.'* It is closer to, "Keep us in your prayers." He offers two motives for their petitions.

(1) The first goal of their prayer is expressed in the un-usual phrase, *'that the word of the Lord may speed on and triumph.'* Perhaps he gets the image from Ps 147:15, which speaks of God's creative word running swiftly to do his work. However, Paul is referring specifically to the gospel proclamation that Jesus Christ is Savior. He personifies the gospel as a messenger and bids them pray that this *'word'* may accomplish the saving task quickly and fully. The image is not that of a race but of an outpouring of power, so that RSV's *'triumph'* is not the best translation. The Greek text has "be glorified," that is, may the word of God display his unique power to accomplish this saving will and bring others to praise him (cf. 1:10, 12 for the compound form of the same verb "glorify").

Ultimately only God can give the gospel message power to touch the hearts of those to whom Paul is now preaching so that *'it may triumph, as it did among you,'* the group he first converted. Gospel preaching has this power because it is "glorified" by God in contrast to all human authority. In the phrase *'speed on and triumph,'* the *'and'* expresses not simple coordination but result. It is equivalent to "and so," that is—may the word of God touch others and so be manifest as the display of God's power.

(2) The second goal that Paul sets for their prayer is for his own support in difficult circumstances. He does not want his recognition that preaching is necessary blind him to the need of God's grace. In the earlier letter he stated that his lot was to be resisted (cf. 1 Thess 3:3). Now he asks their prayers for courage to be *'delivered from wicked and evil men'* so that he and his companions may be faithful to their mission. To which persons does he refer? Paul does not say, but they may be connected to the evil he mentioned above (2:7). If so, this plea for prayers could explain his harsh words about being persecuted by Jews—if they were the ones opposing his Corinthian apostolate (cf. 1 Thess 2:15). The term for *'wicked'* never occurs again in Paul.

In this prayer Paul balances his customary optimism with the realism that *'not all have faith'* (cf. Rom 10:16). But he never abandons his attitude of trust that *'the Lord is faithful'* (cf. 1 Thess 5:24). The *'is'* is emphatic, making the phrase equivalent to, "The Lord is certainly faithful." That fidelity is spelled out in the following statement—a relative clause but translated by an independent clause in RSV—*'he will strengthen you and guard you from evil.'* The word *'strengthen'* is repeated from the prayer immediately above, where it is translated *'establish'* (2:17; Cf. 1 Thess 3:13).

As the RSV marginal note indicates, the final phrase of the sentence may also be translated *'from the evil one.'* In fact, Rigaux states that the meaning *'evil one'* is certain here (cf. 1 Thess 2:18; 3:5; 2 Thess 2:9). The same ambiguity exists in the final petition of Matthew's version of the Lord's prayer (Mt 6:13). Paul is probably thinking of Satan because verses 4 and 5 repeat verbs from his prayer in 1 Thess 3:11-13, which mentions the return of Jesus as judge. Satan is the ultimate inspirer of the evil men who oppose Paul (v.2).

In formulating this implicit petition, Paul has shifted the focus from himself to them, and he uses this shift to reaffirm his confidence in their continued fidelity to *'do the things which we command.'* The verb *'command'* prepares for the next section in which it appears three times (vv.6,10,12; cf. 1 Thess 4:11). Although he speaks gently, Paul is consciously exercising his apostolic authority and his trust that they will respond to God's will for them. He even adds a blessing, as if he were closing the letter. Yet this is not a true final blessing. Rather it is another petition that the *'Lord'* Jesus will make his power available to *'direct your hearts,'* their whole mind and spirit as moral beings (cf. 2:17; 1 Thess 2:17).

Before giving his final directives, Paul again prays for what he prayed for in the beginning of this letter (cf. 1:3-4). He asks that they will have *'the love of God'* to deal with their fellow community members and *'the steadfastness of Christ'* to keep alive their apocalyptic hope. This compressed phrase is to be understood in keeping with the whole tenor of the letter, that is, as expressing Paul's anxiety for them. They need the *'steadfastness'* of Jesus to face opposition and persevere until they share in the victory that he won by his loyalty to his Father.

The same feeling appears in a different context in Paul's earlier letter to them (1 Thess 4:14). For stylistic reasons he refers to Jesus first as *'Lord'* and then as *'Christ.'* Thus he ends this long series of exhortations that he began in 2:13 with the word *'Christ,'* to whom he has referred eight times. By contrast he mentioned God only four times. The emphasis shows that Paul's apocalyptic thrust focused on the return of Jesus.

A CALL FOR WORK.
2 Thess 3:6-15.

> [6]Now we command you, brethren, in the name of our Lord Jesus Christ, that you keep away from any brother who is living in idleness and not in accord with the tradition that you received from us. [7]For you yourselves know how you ought to imitate us; we were not idle when we were with you, [8]we did not eat any one's bread without paying, but with toil and labor we worked night and day, that we might not burden any of you. [9]It was not because we have not that right, but to give you in our conduct an example to imitate. [10]For even when we were with you, we gave you this command: If any one will not work, let him not eat. [11]For we hear that some of you are living in idleness, mere busybodies, not doing any work. [12]Now such persons we command and exhort in the Lord Jesus Christ to do their work in quietness and to earn their own living. [13]Brethren, do not be weary in welldoing.
>
> [14]If any one refuses to obey what we say in this letter, note that man, and have nothing to do with him, that he may be ashamed. [15]Do not look on him as an enemy, but warn him as a brother.

Paul finally comes to the command that he has carefully prepared them to receive. Without mentioning his role as apostole, he exercises his authority to *'command'* them *'in the name of the Lord Jesus Christ.'* Paul is an authorized agent of the risen Jesus commissioned to apply his transcendent power in directing the community. He will avert to this power again at the end of this section by repeating the phrase *'we command . . . in the Lord Jesus Christ'* (v.12). Of the many ways to designate the glorified Jesus, Paul uses the long title *'Lord Jesus Christ'* more than any other New Testament writer (cf. 1:12).

The designation of Jesus as *'Lord'* appears more frequently in this letter than the name *'God'* (22 to 18 times). After 3:5 Paul no longer mentions God. His great emphasis on the role of the risen Jesus is understandable in this letter which urges a strong faith that will enable the community members to persevere until Jesus appears in glory.

Paul's command embraces a twofold prohibition. The community is to *'keep away from'* two classes of people: (1) members *'living in idleness'* and (2) those *'not in accord with the tradition'* he taught them. The Greek adverb translated *'in idleness'* (repeated in v.11) appears nowhere else in the bible. The corresponding verb in verse 7 is likewise used only here in the bible. The word is a general term for disorderly conduct, but the context indicates that their insubordination consists in refusing to work.

This final instruction contains Paul's second appeal to the tradition he taught by his peaching (cf. 2:15). It embraced items both for their instruction and for their personal conduct as believers. In his earlier letter Paul indicated that some unruliness existed in the community but he did not specify it further (1 Thess 5:14). The situation evidently grew worse, forcing Paul to devote this long paragraph to it. His appeal is based on two motives: (1) his own example, highlighted by repeating the verb *'imitate'* (vv.7 and 9), and (2) his earlier instructions to them.

Paul had already offered his own conduct as worthy of their imitation (cf. 1 Thess 1:6; 1 Cor 4:16; Phil 3:17). He is probably contrasting his own productivity for the benefit of the community with the self-centered conduct of the many itinerant preachers of the time who lived off communities they visited (cf. 2 Cor 2:17). *'With toil and labor we worked night and day, that we might not burden any of you'* is almost an exact repetition of what he had written to them before (1 Thess 2:9). When Paul states that he and his fellow evangelists had the *'right'* to be supported, he alludes to a saying of Jesus (cf. Mt 10:10-12; Mk 6:7-11; Lk 9:1-5; 10:3-7; 1 Cor 9:1-23).

By working for a living Paul did not reject the Lord's command but adapted it to concrete circumstances in a way that would foster the spread of the good news. He relies on his apostolic authority in modifying the directives of Jesus to give them, as he puts it, *'in our conduct an example to imitate.'* He implies that even the words of Jesus must be interpreted and applied creatively to serve the needs of the growing community of believers (cf. 1 Thess 1:6-10).

As Paul becomes more involved in this instruction his language grows more personal and once more he uses an idiom of phatic communion *kai gar*, inadequately translated as *'for even.'* The impact of this particle is better rendered by using a question, "Didn't I ... command ...?" (cf. 1 Thess 3:4 for the same idiom). The command, *'If anyone will not work, let him not eat,'* is not found explicitly in his previous letter, but it is intimated there (cf. 1 Thess 4:11-12; 5:14). Obviously this *'command'* is not to be interpreted in wooden fashion. What Paul is doing is to formulate in the form of a proverb a principle of conduct. His readers understand his message: all must assume responsibility for their conduct as members called to a believing community.

Paul makes the nature of this *'command'* clear by explaining what motivates it, namely, to cut off all pretext of adding to the financial burden of the already harried members and to end the threat to community peace or *'quietness'* (cf. 1 Thess 4:11). The verb that appears in English as *'mere busybodies'* is a compound of the verb Paul uses for *'work'* in verse 10. Thus he produces the same play on words other Greek authors used. Paul wants to stress that this command is not anything new; rather, he is recalling previous directives.

He brings this paragraph to a close in a positive manner. First of all, with respect to the overall conduct of the community, he does not want them to *'be weary in well-going,'* that is, to be discouraged in their christian witness (cf. Gal 6:9). More specifically, with respect to those causing this trouble, Paul adopts a twofold approach. On the one hand, they are to be excluded from all community sharing in the hope that they *'may be ashamed'* (cf. 1 Cor 5:9). This is an unusual way of expressing his hope that they will return to the common community practice. This vagueness is favorable to an early dating of the letter; in the early period while community discipline was still developing, terminology was not yet fixed. On the other hand, they must treat each of these idlers not *'as an enemy, but warn him as a brother.'*

Paul thus ends this section that cost him so much agony with the term of mutual love that he used nine times in this letter. To *'warn'* members was one of the functions Paul listed for leaders of the community in his earlier letter; it includes giving instruction (cf. 1 Thess 5:12). He closes his *'command'* with an implicit plea for the cultivation of mutual love that he prayed for in the opening thanksgiving of both letters to the Thessalonians, using the literary technique of an inclusion to round out his message.

FINAL BLESSING.
2 Thess. 3:16-18.

> [16]Now may the Lord of peace himself give you peace at all times in all ways. The Lord be with you all.
> [17]I, Paul write this greeting with my own hand. This is the mark in every letter of mine; it is the way I write.
> [18]The grace of our Lord Jesus Christ be with you all.

For the first of these closing blessings Paul starts with the same formula he used in the blessing in 2:16, *'Now may the Lord . . . himself.'* This formula—which Paul does not use in later letters—appears in 1 Thess 4:16 and, with *'God'* instead of *'Lord'* in 1 Thess 3:11 and 5:23. In the latter blessing Paul invoked *'the God of peace.'* In applying the title *'Lord of peace'* to Jesus (which he does only here), Paul again establishes a functional parallel between the Father and the risen Jesus as agents of salvation. A forger would hardly have invented a new title, but Paul is free enough to create this title in the context of his petition for *'peace at all times in all ways.'* Jesus is the one empowered to communicate God's peace to all.

The addition of another blessing immediately, *'the Lord be with you all,'* seems to be useless repetition. Perhaps it is the overflow of Paul's desire to remind them that the risen Jesus is in command of the world even before he comes again. Thus this blessing could be another reminder of what he had said above, that God himself, through the promises of Jesus, is *'he who now restrains'* the *'son of perdition'* until his saving plan is achieved among the pagans (cf. 2:6).

Such an interpretation could also explain why Paul takes up the writing tool to *'write this greeting with my own hand,'* referring to the blessing that follows. Although the Thessalonians misunderstood some of the instructions in his previous letter, Paul is confident that he has clarified his teaching about how they are to await the coming of the Lord Jesus. He affirms his assurance by the final blessing. But before giving it he reinforces his authority by signing his name and adding, *'it is the way I write.'* The same personal touch appears in 1 Cor 16:21 and Col 4:18 (cf. Gal 6:11). The discovery of manuscripts of letters from the time of Paul indicates that dictated letters often contained the author's signature.

For the third and final time Paul blesses them. This time he uses the same blessing that ended his earlier letter, except for the addition of *'all'* (cf. on 1 Thess 5:28). All three of these blessings are universal in scope. No doubt Paul wants to give a personal example of the advice he just gave them about how to treat recalcitrants, that is, as *'brothers'* in a way that wins them back. The final goal of Christ's work is to save all, no matter how serious the offense. Paul maintains his spirit of hope and confidence that God's saving work in Christ will prevail.

ANNOTATED READING LIST

1. GENERAL READING

John W. Bailey and James W. Clarke, "The First and Second Epistles to the Thessalonians," in *The Interpreter's Bible* Vol. 11, pp. 245-339. Nashville: Abingdon, 1955.

This series is designed for preachers. It gives both the King James and Revised Standard Versions plus a verse by verse exegesis of the text and a homiletic exposition.

Ernest Best, *A Commentary on the First and Second Epistles to the Thessalonians*. New York: Harper and Row, 1972.

This is the most reliable detailed commentary in English. It pays special attention to linguistic problems and to controversial passages and includes a select bibliography.

J. T. Forestell, "The Letters to the Thessalonians," in the *Jerome Biblical Commentary*. Englewood Cliffs, N.J.: Prentice-Hall, 1968.

It provides an introduction and brief comments on verses in the Catholic tradition.

James E. Frame, *Epistles of St. Paul to the Thessalonians*. Edinburgh: T. & T. Clark, 1912.

This old but detailed volume of the International Critical Commentary has been reprinted several times because of its wealth and information.

Kenneth Grayston, *The Letters of Paul to the Philippians and to the Thessalonians*. Cambridge: At the University Press, 1967.

This brief volume of the Cambridge Bible Commentary offers introductory remarks and notes designed to clarify the message of the letters.

William Neil, *St. Paul's Epistles to the Thessalonians*. New York: Macmillan, 1957.

In keeping with the aim of the Torch Bible Commentaries, this volume emphasises the religious significance of these letters.

2. SPECIALISED WORKS

Roger D. Aus, "The Liturgical Background of the Necessity and Propriety of Giving Thanks according to 2 Thess 1:3," *Journal of Biblical Literature* 92 (1973) 432-438.
Liturgical influence explains the special qualities of this unusual form of thanksgiving.

Roger D. Aus, "God's Plan and God's Power: Isaiah 66 and the Restraining Factors of 2 Thess 2:6-7," *Journal of Biblical Literature* 96 (1977) 537-553.
Awareness that this obscure passage alludes to Jewish apocalyptic helps readers grasp its thrust.

H. Boers, "The Form Critical Study of Paul's Letters. 1 Thess as a Case Study," *New Testament Studies* 22 (1975-76) 140-158.
A technical illustration of using form criticism.

R. F. Collins, "The Church of the Thessalonians," *Louvain Studies* 5 (1974-75) 336-349.
A careful examination of 1 Thess to show Paul's early insights into the nature of the church.

L. M. Dewailly, *La jeune église de Thessalonique*. Paris: Cerf, 1963.
Draws out spiritual insights from key passages and themes in these letters.

William G. Doty, *Letters in Primitive Christianity*. Philadelphia: Fortress Press, 1973.
This comprehensive introduction to the formal aspects of New Testament letters shows how they were used in the early church.

Paul Ellingworth and Eugene A. Nida, *A Translator's Handbook on Paul's Letters to the Thessalonians*. Stuttgart: United Bible Societies, 1975.
This volume, using contemporary linguistics to elucidate modes of expressions found in these letters, is invaluable as an aid in grasping Paul's thought.

C. H. Giblin, *The Treat to Faith: An Exegetical and Theological Re-examination of 2 Thessalonians 2.* Rome: Biblical Institute Press, 1967.
A scholarly study that suggests a new approach to this difficult chapter.

R. Jewett, "Enthusiastic Radicalism and the Thessalonian Correspondence," *Society of Biblical Literature 1972 Proceedings*, 181-232.
Argues for the authenticity of 2 Thess as written to clarify misunderstandings arising from 1 Thess.

St. John Chrysostom, "Homilies on the Epistles of St. Paul to the Thessalonians," in the Nicene and Post-Nicene Fathers of the Christian Church series edited by Philip Schiff, Vol. 13, pp. 323-398. New York: Charles Scribner's Sons, 1914.
The exegetical parts of these sermons are still valuable for their explication of Paul's writing.

B. N. Kaye, "Eschatology and Ethics in 1 and 2 Thessalonians," *Novum Testamentum* 17 (1975) 47-57.
Sees little impact of the eschatological stance on the ethical teaching of the letters.

D. W. Kemmler, *Faith and Human Reason: A Study of Paul's Method of Preaching as Illustrated by 1-2 Thessalonians and Acts 17, 2-4.* Leiden: Brill, 1975.
A technical study concentrating on the meaning of words.

Gerhard Krodel, "The 2 Letter to the Thessalonians," (sic) in the Fortress Commentaries series. Philadelphia: Fortress Press, 1978.
The main purpose of this introduction is to prove that 2 Thess is a pseudonymous letter written to preserve the Pauline heritage.

Eugene LaVerdiere, "Introducing First Thessalonians," *The Bible Today* 75 (November 1974) 95-103.
An insightful presentation that is sensitive to Paul's style of writing.

Robert and Carolyn Lee, "An Analysis of the Larger Semantic Units of I Thessalonians," *Notes on Translation* #56 (June 1975) 28-42.
A careful linguistic exposition that offers translators and readers a structural and semantic overview of the letter.

A. Malherbe, "'Gentle as a Nurse': The Cynic Background to I Thess ii," *Novum Testamentum* 12 (1970) 302-317.
Shows the Cynic vocabulary of this chapter and possible implications.

J. Plevnik, "The Parousia as Implication of Christ's Resurrection," in *Lord and Spirit* (D. Stanley volume). Toronto: Regis College, 1975.

B. Rigaux, *Les Épitres aux Thessaloniciens*. Paris: Gabalda, 1956.
Part of the famous Études Bibliques series, this remains the most complete and authoritative commentary on these letters in any language. It is an inexhaustible source of information and a model of critical methodology.

C. J. Roetzel, "1 Thessalonians 5:12-28: A Case Study," *Society of Biblical Literature 1972 Proceedings*, 367-383.
Implications involved in understanding the elements of a Pauline letter.

G. F. Snyder, "Apocalyptic and Didactic Elements in 1 Thessalonians," *Society of Biblical Literature 1972 Proceedings*, 233-244.
In contrast to Kaye's article, holds that the apocalyptic message of Paul carries its own ethical demands.

W. Trilling, *Untersuchungen zum zweiten Thessalonicherbrief*. Leipzig: St. Benno-Verlag, 1972.
Musters arguments against the authenticity of 2 Thess.

NOTES

NOTES

NOTES

NOTES

NOTES

NOTES

NOTES